Kids'
Bible
Questions
& Answers

7

ED STRAUSS

BARBOUR
PUBLISHING

ISBN 978-1-61626-109-2

Published by Barbour Publishing, Inc., P.O. Box 719, Uhrichsville, Ohio 44683, www.barbourbooks.com

Our mission is to publish and distribute inspirational products offering exceptional value and biblical encouragement to the masses.

Printed in the United States of America.
RR Donnelly; Willard, OH 44890; May, 2011; D10002792

CONTENTS

GENESIS 4

EXODUS 17

LEVITICUS 27

NUMBERS 31

DEUTERONOMY 35

JOSHUA 38

JUDGES 43

RUTH 47

1 SAMUEL 49

2 SAMUEL 54

1 KINGS 57

2 KINGS 61

1 CHRONICLES 64

2 CHRONICLES 66

EZRA 69

NEHEMIAH 71

ESTHER .73

JOB 74

PSALMS 75

PROVERBS 80

ECCLESIASTES 81

SONG OF SONGS 83

ISAIAH .84

JEREMIAH 87

LAMENTATIONS 88

EZEKIEL 90

DANIEL .93

JONAH .96

HABAKKUK 97

HAGGAI 98

MATTHEW 99

MARK .106

LUKE 111

JOHN .115

ACTS 120

ROMANS 122

1 CORINTHIANS 124

2 CORINTHIANS 129

GALATIANS 131

EPHESIANS 132

PHILIPPIANS 134

COLOSSIANS 135

1 THESSALONIANS 136

1 TIMOTHY, 2 TIMOTHY 137

TITUS .138

PHILEMON 139

HEBREWS 140

JAMES .142

1 PETER, 2 PETER 143

1 JOHN 144

JUDE 146

REVELATION 147

INDEX .152

WHERE DID GOD COME FROM?

In the beginning God created the heaven and the earth.

GENESIS 1:1 KJV

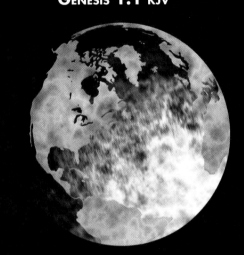

God didn't "come from" anywhere. God has always been around. He has been here forever and will continue to be here forever. This is hard for us to understand, because everything we see around us has a beginning and an ending—even the universe. The first verse in the Bible tells us that God already existed in the beginning, before He created the heavens and the earth (Genesis 1:1). One day, everything we see will come to an end, but God will never end (Psalm 102:27).

God's name in Hebrew is *Yahweh*, which simply means "to exist" or "the Existing One." In other words, God has always existed and He always will. Nobody created God, because no one was around before Him (Isaiah 43:10). King David writes, "Before. . .You had formed the earth and the world, even from everlasting to everlasting, You are God" (Psalm 90:2 NKJV).

The good news is that this means God will always be there for you (Isaiah 46:4)!

COULD GOD REALLY CREATE THE WORLD IN JUST SIX DAYS? ....→

And God saw every thing that he had made, and, behold, it was very good. And the evening and the morning were the sixth day.

GENESIS 1:31 KJV

Yes! Absolutely! In fact, God's power and wisdom are *infinite* (Psalm 147:5)—meaning that they are totally unlimited—so He could have created everything in less time than it takes for you to blink an eye. Think about it: God knows everything that's happening on earth at once. He can concentrate on a billion people praying at one time, so it really would not have been difficult for Him to create all the animals and plants at high speed.

Scientists who don't even believe in God talk about the Big Bang theory, which says that the entire universe, with all the millions of galaxies and billions of stars, came into existence in a fraction of a second. If scientists are convinced that the universe could create *itself* in less than a heartbeat, it shouldn't be difficult to believe that an all-powerful God could create all the galaxies in one day (Genesis 1:14–19) and then create all life on earth in the other five days (Genesis 1–2).

HOW WERE HUMAN BEINGS CREATED? ....

For thousands of years, God's people have believed that God created human beings exactly the way the Bible describes it: On the sixth day of creation, God formed Adam from the dust of the earth and then created Eve from one of Adam's ribs. God could very easily have made men and women that way—and millions of Christians believe that's just how He did it.

However, many other Christians believe that the first chapters of Genesis are symbolic, sort of like parables. They still believe that God created Adam and Eve but think that the "days" of creation were actually periods of millions of years, meaning that humans were created many ages after the animals.

Some churches believe that God created humans through a process called evolution. Whatever your church believes, it's important to know that God is the one who created us, and that He loved us and created this world for us to live in (Isaiah 45:12, 18).

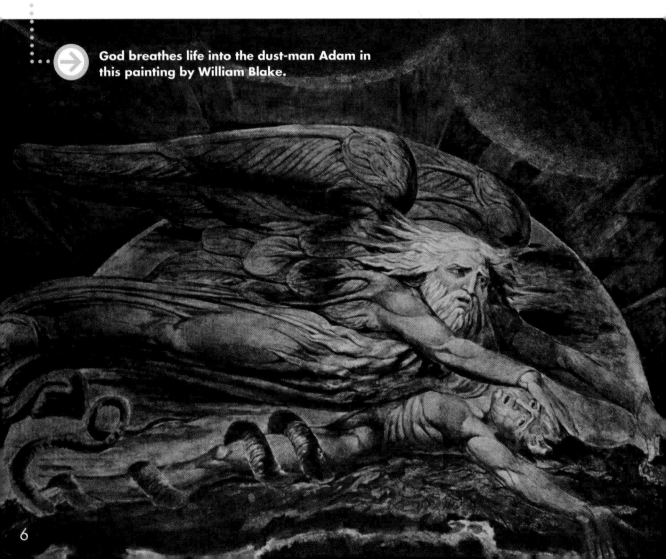

God breathes life into the dust-man Adam in this painting by William Blake.

And God said, Let us make man in our image, after our likeness: and let them have dominion over the fish of the sea, and over the fowl of the air, and over the cattle, and over all the earth, and over every creeping thing that creepeth upon the earth. So God created man in his own image, in the image of God created he him; male and female created he them. . . . And the LORD God said, It is not good that the man should be alone; I will make him an help meet for him. And out of the ground the LORD God formed every beast of the field, and every fowl of the air; and brought them unto Adam to see what he would call them: and whatsoever Adam called every living creature, that was the name thereof. And Adam gave names to all cattle, and to the fowl of the air, and to every beast of the field; but for Adam there was not found an help meet for him. And the LORD God caused a deep sleep to fall upon Adam, and he slept: and he took one of his ribs, and closed up the flesh instead thereof; And the rib, which the LORD God had taken from man, made he a woman, and brought her unto the man. And Adam said, This is now bone of my bones, and flesh of my flesh: she shall be called Woman, because she was taken out of Man.

GENESIS 1:26–27; 2:18–23 KJV

WHY DID GOD HAVE TO REST ON THE SEVENTH DAY?

Thus the heavens and the earth were finished, and all the host of them. And on the seventh day God ended his work which he had made; and he rested on the seventh day from all his work which he had made. And God blessed the seventh day, and sanctified it: because that in it he had rested from all his work which God created and made.

GENESIS 2:1–3 KJV

God didn't *have* to rest the way we need to rest when we're exhausted after a hard day's work. He wasn't tired, because God never becomes weary (Isaiah 40:28).

The Bible says that "on the seventh day God ended His work which he had done, and He rested on the seventh day from all His work" (Genesis 2:2 NKJV). When it says that God "rested," it simply means that He stopped creating. In other words, God stopped working because He had created everything He planned to create. He was done.

God also rested from His work as an example to us. We humans get tired every day and have to sleep at night, but even that isn't enough. We also need to rest one day a week from our schoolwork or jobs. It's fine for us to relax on that day, but God also wants us to use the Sabbath to spend time with Him, read His Word, and recharge our batteries (Exodus 20:8–11).

Doesn't he look tired? Animals and people can get very tired— but God never will!

WHERE EXACTLY WAS THE GARDEN OF EDEN?

The Garden of Eden was, of course, in the land of Eden. In ancient times, Eden was an actual place—but where was it? The Bible says, "The LORD God planted a garden eastward in Eden" (Genesis 2:8 KJV), so we know that Eden was somewhere in the east.

Our best clue is that the Bible says that four rivers came from different directions and joined into one big river, and this river flowed through the land of Eden. It names two of those rivers as the Tigris and the Euphrates (Genesis 2:14). We don't know the identity of the other two rivers, but today the Tigris and the Euphrates flow through the land of Iraq and nearly join before they empty into the Persian Gulf.

Bible scholars believe that, in ancient days, the Tigris and Euphrates actually joined into one river before flowing into the sea. Our best guess is that the Garden of Eden was located in the far southern region of what is today Iraq.

Now the LORD God had planted a garden in the east, in Eden; and there he put the man he had formed. And the LORD God made all kinds of trees grow out of the ground—trees that were pleasing to the eye and good for food. In the middle of the garden were the tree of life and the tree of the knowledge of good and evil. A river watering the garden flowed from Eden; from there it was separated into four headwaters. The name of the first is the Pishon; it winds through the entire land of Havilah, where there is gold. (The gold of that land is good; aromatic resin and onyx are also there.) The name of the second river is the Gihon; it winds through the entire land of Cush. The name of the third river is the Tigris; it runs along the east side of Asshur. And the fourth river is the Euphrates.

GENESIS 2:8–14 NIV

WHO WAS CAIN'S WIFE?...

The Bible says that, at first, Adam and Eve had only two children—Cain and Abel—and Cain killed Abel. Yet after God drove Cain out of Eden and he went to live in Nod, Cain's wife became pregnant. So the question is, Who was Cain's wife if the only human beings on earth at the time were Adam, Eve, and Cain?

> So Cain went out from the LORD's presence and lived in the land of Nod, east of Eden. Cain lay with his wife, and she became pregnant and gave birth to Enoch. Cain was then building a city, and he named it after his son Enoch.
>
> GENESIS 4:16–17 NIV

Eve was "the mother of all the living" (Genesis 3:20), so we know that there weren't any *other* humans on earth except for Eve's descendants. Obviously then, Cain's wife was a daughter of Adam and Eve. Back then, many thousands of years ago, human-kind's DNA wasn't as damaged as it is today, so brothers and sisters could marry.

Also, the Bible lists descendants through the father. This is why sons are named in genealogies (family lists) but almost no daughters are mentioned. Daughters were born as often as sons, and were just as important, but because of the Bible's method of drawing up family trees, daughters (such as Cain's wife) were seldom included.

Most cultures today discourage close relatives from marrying. One of the United States' best-known presidents, Franklin D. Roosevelt, married a relative of his—Eleanor Roosevelt was a distant cousin.

DID PEOPLE IN ANCIENT TIMES ACTUALLY LIVE HUNDREDS OF YEARS?.....

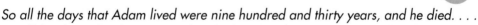

> So all the days that Adam lived were nine hundred and thirty years, and he died. . . .
> So all the days of Seth were nine hundred and twelve years, and he died. . . .
> So all the days of Enosh were nine hundred and five years, and he died. . . .
> So all the days of Kenan were nine hundred and ten years, and he died. . . .
> So all the days of Mahalalel were eight hundred and ninety-five years, and he died. . . .
> So all the days of Jared were nine hundred and sixty-two years, and he died. . . .
> So all the days of Methuselah were nine hundred and sixty-nine years, and he died.
>
> GENESIS 5:5, 8, 11, 14, 17, 20, 27 NASB

Yes, they did. Before the flood of Noah's day, people lived for many centuries. For example, Adam lived to be 930 years of age, and Methuselah, the oldest man on record, died at age 969 (Genesis 5:5, 27). We shouldn't be surprised by this. Even today, Sequoia redwood trees can live 2,500 years. Since human beings were God's greatest creation, He wanted them to live a long time too.

But something happened after the Flood. Maybe it was changes in the earth, or perhaps sin had greatly damaged humankind's DNA, but gradually people began living shorter lives. After the Flood, Shem lived only 600 years, Arphaxad lived just 438 years, Peleg lived a mere 239 years, and Terah died of old age at 205. Abraham lived 175 years, Jacob lived 147 years, and Joseph lived 110 years (Genesis 11:10–32; 25:7; 47:28; 50:26).

By King David's day, three thousand years ago, people were living only seventy or eighty years (Psalm 90:10), just like today.

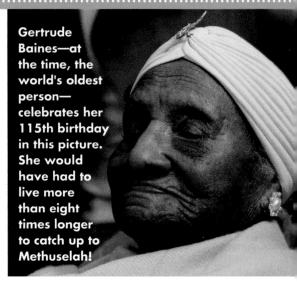

Gertrude Baines—at the time, the world's oldest person—celebrates her 115th birthday in this picture. She would have had to live more than eight times longer to catch up to Methuselah!

HOW COULD TWO OF EVERY SPECIES OF ANIMAL FIT INTO NOAH'S ARK?....... ⮕

First of all, the ark was not small. It was a massive ship—450 feet long, 75 feet wide, and 45 feet tall; and it had three decks (each one 15 feet high) to house all the animals (Genesis 6:15–16).

Second, God told Noah to bring two of every species of animal onto the ark (Genesis 6:19–20). All the hundreds of breeds of dogs in the world today are not separate species. All dogs are descended from a common ancestor—wolves—so Noah only needed to take two wolves on board. It was the same with cows, horses, and so on.

Then Noah and his sons and his wife and his sons' wives with him entered the ark because of the water of the flood. Of clean animals and animals that are not clean and birds and everything that creeps on the ground, there went into the ark to Noah by twos, male and female, as God had commanded Noah.

GENESIS 7:7–9 NASB

Third, while some animals, such as elephants and rhinos, are huge, most animals are smaller. The average animal is only about the size of a sheep. Birds and hamsters and butterflies are *very* small indeed.

Fourth, Noah didn't need to take any fish or sea creatures on board. They survived just fine out in the ocean.

⮕ This model of Noah's Ark gives a sense of how big it was—check out the elephants and giraffes lining up in front!

WHY DID GOD PROMISE THE LAND OF CANAAN TO ABRAHAM WHEN IT ALREADY BELONGED TO THE CANAANITES?

When Abraham (also called Abram) arrived in Canaan, the Bible says, "At that time the Canaanites were in the land. The LORD appeared to Abram and said, 'To your offspring I will give this land'" (Genesis 12:6–7 NIV).

The land didn't belong to the Canaanites. They were there, yes, but they'd moved in without permission. To whom did the land belong? It belonged to God; and because it was His, He could give it to the Israelites. Just the same, He made it clear even to Israel: "The land is Mine; for you are strangers and sojourners with Me" (Leviticus 25:23 NKJV).

Because it was God's land, only God's people had the right to live there. The Canaanites were a wicked people and had no business being there. God said that they "defiled the land" and that the land itself would "vomit them out" (Leviticus 18:24–28; Ezra 9:11) so that God's people could move in.

> Abram passed through the land to the place of Shechem, as far as the terebinth tree of Moreh. And the Canaanites were then in the land. Then the LORD appeared to Abram and said, "To your descendants I will give this land." And there he built an altar to the LORD, who had appeared to him.
>
> GENESIS 12:6–7 NKJV

Unlike the Middle East, where people have been fighting for land for thousands of years, the United States welcomes newcomers. A poem on a bronze plaque at the Statue of Liberty reads, "Give me your tired, your poor, your huddled masses yearning to breathe free. . . ."

IF ABRAHAM WAS SUCH A GREAT MAN, WHY DID HE LIE THAT HIS WIFE, SARAH, WAS ONLY HIS SISTER?..........

Abraham was a righteous man, and the most outstanding thing about Abraham was that he had such great faith. God promised Abraham that he would have as many descendants as the stars of the sky, and even though it seemed impossible, Abraham believed God (Genesis 15:2–6). Read Romans 4:18–22 to see just how strong his faith was!

Yet Abraham was only human, and he had weaknesses, too. His wife, Sarah, was so beautiful that Abraham was frightened that some ruthless king would kill him so he could take Sarah as a wife. That's why Abraham told Pharaoh that Sarah was just his sister (Genesis 12:10–20).

Later, God told him, "Do not be afraid, Abram. I am your shield." But the next time Abraham was faced with a dangerous situation, he gave in to his fears again and stopped trusting God (Genesis 15:1; 20:1–18). This is a lesson for all of us: Trust God and *keep* trusting God!

→ We all get nervous and scared sometimes. . .but the Bible says that God didn't give us a spirit of fear, "but of power, and of love, and of a sound mind" (2 TIMOTHY 1:7 KJV).

→ Now there was a famine in the land, and Abram went down to Egypt to dwell there, for the famine was severe in the land. And it came to pass, when he was close to entering Egypt, that he said to Sarai his wife, "Indeed I know that you are a woman of beautiful countenance. Therefore it will happen, when the Egyptians see you, that they will say, This is his wife'; and they will kill me, but they will let you live. Please say you are my sister, that it may be well with me for your sake, and that I may live because of you." So it was, when Abram came into Egypt, that the Egyptians saw the woman, that she was very beautiful. The princes of Pharaoh also saw her and commended her to Pharaoh. And the woman was taken to Pharaoh's house. He treated Abram well for her sake. He had sheep, oxen, male donkeys, male and female servants, female donkeys, and camels. But the LORD plagued Pharaoh and his house with great plagues because of Sarai, Abram's wife. And Pharaoh called Abram and said, "What is this you have done to me? Why did you not tell me that she was your wife? Why did you say, 'She is my sister'? I might have taken her as my wife. Now therefore, here is your wife; take her and go your way." So Pharaoh commanded his men concerning him; and they sent him away, with his wife and all that he had.

GENESIS 12:10–20 NKJV

WHY DID GOD TELL ABRAHAM TO SACRIFICE (KILL) HIS SON ISAAC? ......⊕

Now it came to pass after these things that God tested Abraham, and said to him, "Abraham!" And he said, "Here I am." Then He said, "Take now your son, your only son Isaac, whom you love, and go to the land of Moriah, and offer him there as a burnt offering on one of the mountains of which I shall tell you."

GENESIS 22:1–2 NKJV

God had just done a miracle to give Abraham and Sarah a son in their old age, and Abraham loved Isaac dearly because he was his very own son. Also, he knew that this miracle child would now inherit all the promises that God had given to him. So you can imagine how shocked Abraham was when God asked him to sacrifice Isaac!

Abraham didn't know it at the time, but God had no intention of letting him kill his son. He wanted to test Abraham's love and obedience. Sure enough, when Abraham showed that he was willing to give his beloved son to God, God responded immediately. He called Abraham's name *twice* to make sure to stop him; then—to be certain that Abraham understood clearly—God told him *twice* not to harm his son. And then God blessed Abraham with three fantastic blessings at once.

When Abraham obeyed God, Isaac lived. If Abraham had disobeyed God, Isaac still would have lived, but both father and son would have missed the blessings that God intended for them. Either way, though, Isaac was in no danger of being killed by Abraham.

An angel stops Abraham from killing Isaac in this classic 1635 painting by Rembrandt.

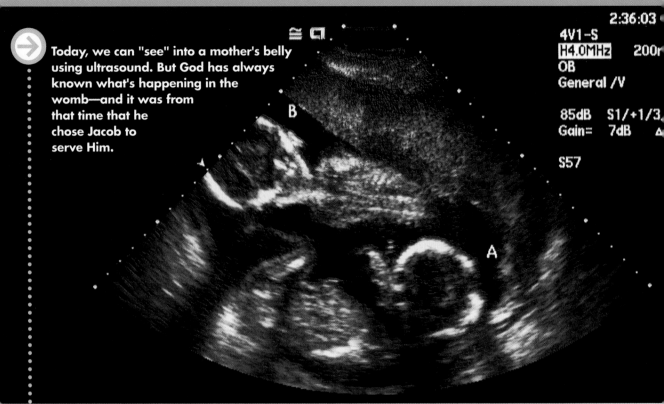

Today, we can "see" into a mother's belly using ultrasound. But God has always known what's happening in the womb—and it was from that time that he chose Jacob to serve Him.

2:36:03

4V1-S
H4.0MHz   200r
OB
General /V

85dB   S1/+1/3
Gain=   7dB

S57

WHY DID GOD CHOOSE JACOB OVER ESAU BEFORE EITHER SON WAS EVEN BORN?..............

Before Jacob and Esau were even born—before they had done anything good or evil—God told their mother, Rebekah, "The older shall serve the younger" (Genesis 25:23; Romans 9:10–12 NKJV). In other words, the youngest twin would inherit the promises God had made to Abraham and would be the father of God's people, Israel.

> The LORD said to her, "Two nations are in your womb, and two peoples from within you will be separated; one people will be stronger than the other, and the older will serve the younger."
>
> GENESIS 25:23 TNIV

Most Christians believe that because God knows everything—even the future—He knew exactly what kind of terrible, selfish choices Esau (the older son) would make. That's why He didn't choose Esau to inherit the promises.

Or perhaps Esau just wasn't the kind of person God was looking for. Esau was strong physically, headstrong, and warlike, whereas Jacob was weaker and meeker. Why on earth would God choose Jacob? Because He knew that Jacob would have to trust Him more than strong, able Esau—and thus God would get the credit for doing miracles. "God has chosen the weak things of the world to put to shame the things which are mighty. . .that no flesh should glory in His presence" (1 Corinthians 1:27, 29 NKJV).

WHY DID REBEKAH AND JACOB DECEIVE ISAAC? WAS IT RIGHT?.............→

When Isaac's wife, Rebekah, became pregnant with twins, God told her, "The older shall serve the younger" (Genesis 25:23 NKJV). Isaac apparently didn't believe that God had spoken to his wife. Even after Esau sold his birthright to Jacob (Genesis 25:29–34), Isaac still favored Esau. For nearly 80 years, year after year, Rebekah probably reminded Isaac what God had said, but Isaac refused to change his mind.

Finally, the day came when Isaac prepared to bless Esau in the traditional manner—which was the *opposite* of what God had said would happen. Rebekah must have panicked, because she disguised Jacob as Esau and sent him into Isaac's tent pretending that he was Esau. Because Isaac was blind, the trick worked, and once Isaac had given Jacob his blessing, he couldn't take it back and give it to Esau.

> After Isaac finished blessing him, and Jacob had scarcely left his father's presence, his brother Esau came in from hunting. He too prepared some tasty food and brought it to his father. Then he said to him, "My father, please sit up and eat some of my game, so that you may give me your blessing." His father Isaac asked him, "Who are you?" "I am your son," he answered, "your firstborn, Esau." Isaac trembled violently and said, "Who was it, then, that hunted game and brought it to me? I ate it just before you came and I blessed him—and indeed he will be blessed!"
>
> GENESIS 27:30–33 TNIV

Isaac's stubborn disbelief was wrong, but Rebekah's deception was wrong also. God wanted Jacob to receive the blessing, but He could have worked out a different solution to the problem.

→ Jacob and his mother, Rebekah, trick old Isaac into giving his younger son the blessing his firstborn should have gotten. This painting is from 1638.

WHY DID JOSEPH'S BROTHERS HATE HIM AND SELL HIM AS A SLAVE?.......................

God gave Jacob 12 sons but chose one of Jacob's youngest sons, Joseph, for great things. God then pre-pared Joseph for his future by giving him dreams that one day his older brothers would bow down to him. Joseph should have kept his dreams to himself, or per-haps told only his father, but he couldn't resist boasting to his brothers. That made them *so* mad! On top of it, Jacob spoiled Joseph by giving him—and *only* him—a beautiful, expensive coat. You can see why his brothers were jealous.

Still, this was no excuse for their wanting to kill Joseph. Fortunately, they spared his life and sold him as a slave into Egypt instead. Once there, Joseph be-came a powerful ruler and saved many countries from a great famine.

This is one of those amazing stories in which people act in anger and jealousy, but God—in His love and great power—turns a bad situation around and makes good come out of it (Genesis 45:4–8).

They spotted him off in the distance. By the time he got to them they had cooked up a plot to kill him. The brothers were saying, "Here comes that dreamer. Let's kill him and throw him into one of these old cisterns; we can say that a vicious animal ate him up. We'll see what his dreams amount to." Reuben heard the brothers talking and intervened to save him, "We're not going to kill him. No murder. Go ahead and throw him in this cistern out here in the wild, but don't hurt him." Reuben planned to go back later and get him out and take him back to his father. When Joseph reached his brothers, they ripped off the fancy coat he was wearing, grabbed him, and threw him into a cistern. The cistern was dry; there wasn't any water in it. Then they sat down to eat their supper. Looking up, they saw a caravan of Ishmaelites on their way from Gilead, their camels loaded with spices, ointments, and perfumes to sell in Egypt. Judah said, "Brothers, what are we going to get out of killing our brother and concealing the evidence? Let's sell him to the Ishmaelites, but let's not kill him—he is, after all, our brother, our own flesh and blood." His brothers agreed.

GENESIS 37:18–27 MSG

In a 1630 painting, Diego Velazquez didn't make Joseph's coat very colorful...but he shows how Joseph's brothers dipped the coat in animal blood to make their father, Jacob, believe his son had been killed by a wild animal. Read the story in Genesis 37:31–34.

WHY DID GOD APPEAR AS A BURNING A BUSH?

When Moses first saw a bush burning near Mount Horeb, he probably thought that someone had lit it or that perhaps lightning had started a fire. But as he kept watching, he noticed that the fire didn't burn out. The bush was still there! Moses then went over to investigate. So part of the reason God appeared that way was to get Moses' attention.

But why would God appear as fire? Why didn't He let Moses see what He actually looked like? God couldn't do that. Later on, when Moses begged God, "Please, show me Your glory," God replied, "You cannot see My face; for no man shall see Me, and live" (Exodus 33:18–23 NKJV). God is too glorious and awesome for human eyes to look upon. It would have been more devastating to Moses than staring at the sun.

This was the same reason that God appeared to the Israelites in a pillar of cloud and fire (Exodus 33:7–11).

Moses was shepherding the flock of Jethro, his father-in-law, the priest of Midian. He led the flock to the west end of the wilderness and came to the mountain of God, Horeb. The angel of GOD appeared to him in flames of fire blazing out of the middle of a bush. He looked. The bush was blazing away but it didn't burn up. Moses said, "What's going on here? I can't believe this! Amazing! Why doesn't the bush burn up?" GOD saw that he had stopped to look. God called to him from out of the bush, "Moses! Moses!" He said, "Yes? I'm right here!"
EXODUS 3:1–4 MSG

This bright red plant is called a "burning bush"— but the one Moses saw was actually on fire with God's presence!

DOES GOD STILL SPEAK TO PEOPLE OUT LOUD AS HE DID TO MOSES?

The Bible doesn't say that God always spoke to Moses in an audible (out loud) voice. Certainly He did at times. When the Israelites arrived at Mount Sinai, "Moses spoke, and God answered him by voice" (Exodus 19:19 NKJV). However God spoke to Moses, we know that God spoke to him clearly and in great detail.

> God said to Moses, "I AM WHO I AM"; and He said, "Thus you shall say to the sons of Israel, 'I AM has sent me to you.'"
>
> EXODUS 3:14 NASB

God also spoke out loud to Jesus; but even though an entire crowd heard a voice from heaven, many thought it was an angel speaking. Some who weren't spiritually sensitive thought that it had simply thundered (John 12:28–29).

It would be very rare for God to speak to people out loud today. Instead, most Christians sense God speaking to them as they read the Bible. It is God's Word, after all. Sometimes a specific verse grabs their attention. Other times, God communicates with people through their conscience or intuition. Many Christians believe they have heard God speak in a "still small voice" in their minds (1 Kings 19:12 NKJV).

WHY WAS THE FIRST-BORN SON SO SPECIAL?...

Among the ancient Hebrews, the first signs of new life—whether plant, animal, or human—were seen as the beginning of God's creative power. They understood that this first new life belonged to God and should be given back to Him. Thus, the Hebrews always gave the best of the *firstfruits* (the first ripened fruit or crop) to God (Exodus 23:16). They also knew that the firstborn of their animals were God's, which is why they sacrificed them to Him (Exodus 34:19).

This was also true for a man and woman's first son: He belonged to God (Exodus 13:1–2). Of course, God didn't expect parents to sacrifice their sons, which is why He told them to redeem (buy back) their firstborn by sacrificing a lamb (Exodus 13:11–15; Leviticus 12:6–8). Even Jesus' parents redeemed Him (Luke 2:22–24).

In Israelite society, the firstborn son had special responsibilities and rights; after his father died, he was given twice as big an inheritance as his younger brothers and was expected to lead the family.

There's still something special about a family's first baby!

"Now when the LORD brings you to the land of the Canaanite, as He swore to you and to your fathers, and gives it to you, you shall devote to the LORD the first offspring of every womb, and the first offspring of every beast that you own; the males belong to the LORD. But every first offspring of a donkey you shall redeem with a lamb, but if you do not redeem it, then you shall break its neck; and every firstborn of man among your sons you shall redeem. And it shall be when your son asks you in time to come, saying, 'What is this?' then you shall say to him, 'With a powerful hand the LORD brought us out of Egypt, from the house of slavery. It came about, when Pharaoh was stubborn about letting us go, that the LORD killed every firstborn in the land of Egypt, both the firstborn of man and the firstborn of beast. Therefore, I sacrifice to the LORD the males, the first offspring of every womb, but every firstborn of my sons I redeem.'"

EXODUS 13:11–15 NASB

HOW DID GOD PART THE RED SEA?.......

The Bible says, "The LORD drove the sea back by a strong east wind all night," and when the Israelites crossed on the dry sea bed, the water was like a *wall* on their right and left hands (Exodus 14:21–22 RSV). Normally, a wind with enough force to part the seas would also have picked up the Israelites and hurled them through the air violently—so the wind couldn't have been *too* strong.

The key to understanding this mystery is found a few verses later, where Moses, an eyewitness to the miracle, says, "The floods stood upright like a heap; the depths congealed in the heart of the sea" (Exodus 15:8 NKJV). The word *congealed* means "hardened."

So the wind wasn't just blowing the sea apart; the water had been hardened and made solid, like walls. That doesn't mean the Red Sea was frozen like ice, but to say that the water "congealed" does mean that something very strange happened. The normal laws of nature were bent to the miracle-working power of God.

Then Moses stretched out his hand over the sea, and all that night the LORD drove the sea back with a strong east wind and turned it into dry land. The waters were divided, and the Israelites went through the sea on dry ground, with a wall of water on their right and on their left.

EXODUS 14:21–22 NIV

The bright coral reef and fish here were photographed in the waters of the Red Sea. . . . Do you think Moses and the people of Israel might have seen something like this through those walls of water they walked between?

WHY DiD THE CHiLDREN OF iSRAEL COMPLAIN SO MUCH RiGHT AFTER GOD HAD DONE AMAZiNG MiRACLES FOR THEM?

God did a huge miracle by parting the Red Sea for the Israelites. Three days later, at Marah, God made bitter water drinkable (Exodus 14–15). But now the Israelites were in the desert and hungry and they complained that God had brought them out there just to let them starve. What a lack of trust! God promptly did a miracle and supplied them with manna for the next 40 years (Exodus 16:1–12).

When we look back at the whole story from beginning to end, it's easy to see that God was ready to do miracles for the Israelites and that they should have continued to trust Him and have patience. God loved them and was not about to abandon them. Yet when we get in difficult situations ourselves, *our* faith gets tested, too. We remember that God has done good things for us, but when new difficulties arise, we can easily forget His past miracles and wonder whether God is powerful enough to take care of us *now*. We may even doubt whether He loves us enough to help us. Rather than judging the children of Israel, we should learn lessons from what they did.

Complaining is never pretty. . . and the Bible often warns against it!

And the whole congregation of the people of Israel murmured against Moses and Aaron in the wilderness, and said to them, "Would that we had died by the hand of the LORD in the land of Egypt, when we sat by the fleshpots and ate bread to the full; for you have brought us out into this wilderness to kill this whole assembly with hunger."

EXODUS 16:2–3 RSV

DO WE STiLL NEED TO OBEY THE TEN COMMANDMENTS TODAY?

Yes, we should certainly obey the Ten Commandments. They instruct us to do good things, such as worshipping God only. What Christian would think that it's no longer important to love and worship God? And of course we should obey the commands not to lie, steal, or kill. All these are vitally important rules.

But much of the *rest* of the detailed Law of Moses no

longer applies. Since Jesus, the Lamb of God, died as the perfect sacrifice (John 1:29; 1 Peter 1:18–19), believers no longer need to sacrifice animals to take away their sins. We don't need to follow all the ceremonial laws or go through endless rituals to stay clean. But the Ten Commandments still apply.

Remember, however, that Jesus said that the most *important* commands are to love God with all our hearts and to love our neighbors as ourselves (Matthew 22:36–40). The good news is that if we keep these two commands, we're already fulfilling the Ten Commandments (Romans 13:8–10).

Moses carries the Ten Commandments down Mount Sinai in this classic engraving from the 1800s.

"Worship no god but me. Do not make for yourselves images of anything in heaven or on earth or in the water under the earth. Do not bow down to any idol or worship it, because I am the Lord your God and I tolerate no rivals. I bring punishment on those who hate me and on their descendants down to the third and fourth generation. But I show my love to thousands of generations of those who love me and obey my laws. Do not use my name for evil purposes, for I, the Lord your God, will punish anyone who misuses my name. Observe the Sabbath and keep it holy. You have six days in which to do your work, but the seventh day is a day of rest dedicated to me. On that day no one is to work—neither you, your children, your slaves, your animals, nor the foreigners who live in your country. In six days I, the Lord, made the earth, the sky, the seas, and everything in them, but on the seventh day I rested. That is why I, the Lord, blessed the Sabbath and made it holy. Respect your father and your mother, so that you may live a long time in the land that I am giving you. Do not commit murder. Do not commit adultery. Do not steal. Do not accuse anyone falsely. Do not desire another man's house; do not desire his wife, his slaves, his cattle, his donkeys, or anything else that he owns."

EXODUS 20:3–17 GNT

DOES GOD REALLY PUNISH CHILDREN FOR THEIR PARENTS' SINS?.....

In the Ten Commandments, the first command is to worship God only. The second command is also vitally important: The Israelites were not to make idols or worship other gods—which were actually demons (1 Corinthians 10:19–20). Idolatry was so damaging and evil that God added, "For I the LORD thy God am a jealous God, visiting the iniquity of the fathers upon the children unto the third and fourth generation of them that hate me" (Exodus 20:5 KJV).

> *"You shall not bow down to them nor serve them. For I, the LORD your God, am a jealous God, visiting the iniquity of the fathers upon the children to the third and fourth generations of those who hate Me, but showing mercy to thousands, to those who love Me and keep My commandments."*
>
> EXODUS 20:5–6 NKJV

When people hated God, worshipped demons, and taught their children to hate God and worship demons, it often affected families for generations. And as long as the children continued in their parents' sins, yes, God continued to judge them, too.

Later, some Israelites claimed that they were innocent but that God was judging them for their fathers' sins. God told them to stop saying that and explained that no matter how bad their fathers had been, if *they* would do what was right and not worship idols, He would bless them (Ezekiel 18:1–9).

WHAT DOES IT MEAN TO TAKE GOD'S NAME IN VAIN?.....

> "Be careful, little lips, what you say" is what an old Sunday school song warned. God is very particular about how His name is spoken!

!#?@!

> *Thou shalt not take the name of the LORD thy God in vain; for the LORD will not hold him guiltless that taketh his name in vain.*
>
> EXODUS 20:7 KJV

The third commandment says, "You shall not take the name of the LORD your God in vain" (Exodus 20:7 NKJV). To use God's name "in vain" means to speak it in the wrong way or to carelessly say that God will do things that God would actually not do.

The NIV translation says, "You shall not misuse the name of the LORD your God." You hear a lot of people misuse God's name these days. Whenever they are hateful or angry, they use God's name to curse others, or want God to judge or damn somebody to hell.

People who do this are showing a great lack of respect and love for God and a lack of respect and love for other people. They are not only breaking the third commandment, but also breaking the two most important commands in the Bible: to love God with all their hearts and to love their neighbor as themselves (Matthew 22:36–40).

WHY DO SOME CHRISTIANS REST ON SATURDAY AND OTHERS REST ON SUNDAY?

When God said, "Remember the Sabbath day, to keep it holy" (Exodus 20:8 RSV), He explained that His people should do all their work during six days and rest on the seventh day. This was because God created the world in six days but ceased from work on the seventh day. Because Saturday was the last day of the week, the Jews celebrated Sabbath on Saturday—and still do.

"Observe the Sabbath day, to keep it holy. Work six days and do everything you need to do. But the seventh day is a Sabbath to GOD, your God. Don't do any work—not you, nor your son, nor your daughter, nor your servant, nor your maid, nor your animals, not even the foreign guest visiting in your town. For in six days GOD made Heaven, Earth, and sea, and everything in them; he rested on the seventh day. Therefore GOD blessed the Sabbath day; he set it apart as a holy day."

EXODUS 20:8–10 MSG

For this reason, some Christians also rest on Saturday; but for two thousand years, most Christians have rested on Sunday. This is because Jesus was raised back to life on a Sunday, the first day of the week (John 20:1). Christians considered the Resurrection to be such an important event that they began to rest on Sundays instead. The early church gathered together to "break bread" (celebrate the Lord's Supper) and meet every Sunday (Acts 20:7; 1 Corinthians 16:2).

"Day of rest" doesn't mean you have to sleep the whole time—but God does want you to slow down, rest, and think of Him more.

WHAT WAS THE ARK OF THE COVENANT, AND WHAT MADE IT SO SPECIAL?.....

The original ark disappeared centuries ago—but this model is based on the Bible's description of the special box. From under those cherubim angels' wings, God would actually speak to the high priest of Israel!

"Make a Box out of acacia wood, 45 inches long, 27 inches wide, and 27 inches high. Cover it with pure gold inside and out and put a gold border all around it."

EXODUS 25:10–11 GNT

The ark of the covenant was a small chest made out of acacia wood and covered with gold, both inside and out. A golden lid, called the atonement cover, was placed on top of the ark, with two golden cherubim with outspread wings on top of that. The two stone tablets of the Law, a gold jar of manna, and Aaron's rod were stored inside the ark (Hebrews 9:4).

When the Israelites were in the wilderness, the ark was kept inside the Tent of Meeting. When Solomon built a permanent temple in Jerusalem, the ark was kept in the heart of the temple, in a special room called the Holy of Holies.

God did not live permanently in, or on, the ark, but He sometimes appeared between the two golden cherubim and spoke from there (Exodus 25:22). That's why the Israelites considered the ark to be a symbol of the presence of God and treated it as a holy object.

WHAT WAS THE TABERNACLE?..........

When the children of Israel wandered in the desert for 40 years, they needed a place where they could worship God and offer sacrifices to Him. And they had to be able to pack it up and carry it along with them when they moved. So

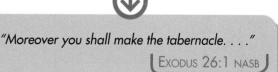

"Moreover you shall make the tabernacle. . . ."

EXODUS 26:1 NASB

instead of building a temple of stone, they built a large tent and surrounded it with a tall cloth wall. *Tabernacle* is an Old English word that means "tent" or "meeting-place tent," which is why some Bible translations call the tabernacle the Tent of Meeting.

The ark of the covenant and other holy articles were kept inside the tabernacle. The Israelites went to the tabernacle to ask God questions, and God often descended in a pillar of cloud and fire and met with Moses there (Exodus 33:7–11).

For hundreds of years after they settled in Canaan, the Israelites still worshipped at the Tent of Meeting. Finally, King Solomon built a permanent stone temple.

This sketch of the tabernacle shows the outer "walls" of cloth hung on poles, and the inner tent where the priest would meet with God. Sacrifices were made on the altar in front of the tent.

DOES GOD HAVE A BODY LIKE WE DO?....⬇

God is a spirit (John 4:24), so He doesn't have a physical body like ours. A physical body can be in only one place at a time. That, of course, would limit God, and the Bible tells us that God has no limits. He is *omnipresent*, which means that He is everywhere at once (Psalm 139:7–10). God is so vast, in fact, that even the universe itself can't contain Him (2 Chronicles 2:6).

Nevertheless, if God so chooses, He *can* take on a form like a human body. When He appeared to Moses, God had a face, hands, and a back (Exodus 33:20–23). Mind you, God can *also* appear as the flame in a burning bush or a pillar of cloud and fire instead (Exodus 3:2–6; 13:20–21). God is simply not limited.

Many Christian scholars teach that each time God appeared in a human body, it was actually God's Son, Jesus, who appeared. God the Father, Jesus, and the Holy Spirit are all part of God, but Jesus is the only one who actually has a physical body. Jesus could do this because He is God, so He has always existed, even before He was born physically.

"Then I will remove my hand and you will see my back; but my face must not be seen."
Exodus 33:23 NIV

You've probably seen pictures—like this classic painting by Michelangelo—of God as a stern, white-haired man. But that's just an artist's idea.

WHY DID GOD GIVE THE ISRAELITES SO MANY RULES AND LAWS TO FOLLOW?

God gave the Israelites many rules to teach them how to serve Him, how to come into His presence with respect, and how to sacrifice to Him the right way. Because God is all-powerful and holy, the Israelites needed to respect and worship Him. They could not afford to approach God flippantly and carelessly.

Also, many of the laws that God gave were practical laws about how to farm, how to settle unsolved murders, how to provide for the poor, how to treat foreigners, how to hold fair court cases, and how to give just punishments for crimes. Israel was a brand-new nation and needed rules to govern them, so God gave them many helpful laws. (We have many *more* laws in modern times.)

NO
FISHING
CRABBING
ROLLERSKATES
BICYCLES

The Lord called to Moses from the Tent of the Lord's presence and gave him the following rules. . . .
LEVITICUS 1:1 GNT

Does it ever seem like everyone's telling you "No"? Even the Bible can seem that way sometimes—but all those rules were designed to give people a better, happier life.

AFTER THEY HAD SINNED, WHY DID THE ISRAELITES HAVE TO SACRIFICE AN ANIMAL?

The Law of Moses said that anyone who sinned and broke the Lord's commands had to bring an animal (a bull or a goat) to the Lord's altar and sacrifice (kill) it. This was called a sin offering (Leviticus 4).

When a sin had been committed, the penalty for sin was death. The Bible says, "Blood, which is life,

> "He shall lay his hand on the head of the sin offering, and kill the sin offering in the place of burnt offering."
> LEVITICUS 4:29 RSV

takes away sins," and "Sins are forgiven only if blood is poured out" (Leviticus 17:11; Hebrews 9:22 GNT). However, instead of dying for their sins, the people could repent and bring a bull or a goat to sacrifice instead.

God did the same thing when He told the Israelites to sacrifice a lamb at Passover and sprinkle its blood on their doorposts (Exodus 12). Finally, Jesus was the Lamb of God (John 1:29) who died at Passover for the sins of the world. After Jesus' blood was poured out to cover our sins once and for all, there was no longer any need for animal sacrifices.

Lambs—cute little guys like this—paid a high price for people's sin in Old Testament times. But animal sacrifices came to an end when Jesus—"the Lamb of God"—died on the cross. His sacrifice was enough to cover every sin, of every person, for all time!

WHY DID THE ISRAELITES HAVE SO MANY RULES ABOUT FOOD, AND WHY DON'T CHRISTIANS FOLLOW THESE DIETARY LAWS TODAY?

There were practical reasons for God's health laws. Most of the animals on God's do-not-eat list are scavengers—animals such as vultures and other carrion-eaters—and their meat is full of diseases. Pigs eat just about anything, too, and pork can make you sick if it's not cooked properly. Many kinds of (nonfish) sea creatures are scavengers, too.

Many Christians believe that the laws about clean and unclean foods are no longer in

> "These are the regulations concerning animals, birds, every living thing that moves in the water and every creature that moves about on the ground. You must distinguish between the unclean and the clean, between living creatures that may be eaten and those that may not be eaten."
> LEVITICUS 11:46–47 TNIV

effect, since God gave Peter a vision in Acts 10:9–16 (NIV) about a sheet full of all kinds of unclean animals and told him, "Get up, Peter. Kill and eat."

Other Christians say that Peter's vision wasn't actually about food, but that the unclean beasts symbolized the unclean Gentiles, whom God was now accepting (Acts 10:13–15, 28). They believe that God's food laws still apply.

Ultimately, what we choose to eat is a matter of conscience. Whatever you believe, remember, don't judge others because of what they eat or don't eat (Romans 14:1–3).

Who'd want to eat that nasty vulture—especially when you know the gross stuff he's been feeding on? God's laws said "No" to eating vultures—but also to much tastier dishes like

WHY DiD THE iSRAELiTES HAVE TO CELEBRATE SO MANY FESTiVALS EACH YEAR?.........⬇

Most of the Israelites' festivals were a time for the people to rest from their work, celebrate, and have feasts. They looked forward to these holidays.

For us today, Christmas and Easter are special dates when we pause to remember that God sent Jesus and raised Him from the dead. Just so, at the Passover feast, or seder, the Israelites remembered how

GOD spoke to Moses: "Tell the People of Israel, These are my appointed feasts, the appointed feasts of GOD which you are to decree as sacred assemblies. . . ."

LEVITICUS 23:1-2 MSG

→ A Jewish family celebrates Passover, as Jewish families have been doing for more than 3,000 years!

God delivered them from slavery in Egypt. The Feast of Tabernacles reminded them how God had cared for them for 40 years in the wilderness.

At Thanksgiving (after harvest), we thank God for providing for us during the past year. The Israelites had two harvest festivals—the Feast of Firstfruits and the Feast of Weeks, when people showed their thankfulness by giving God offerings

from their crops and vineyards.

And just as we have a serious holiday, Memorial Day, to honor soldiers who have died in our nation's wars, the Jews had a serious festival called the Day of Atonement, when they remembered their sins and trusted God to forgive them.

WERE MEN WORTH MORE THAN WOMEN IN OLD TESTAMENT TIMES?.... →

In ancient Israel, sometimes a man would dedicate certain family members to the Lord. Later on, however, they might be needed again to help support the family. In those cases, their family would have to redeem them (buy them back) from the Lord so they could work for the family again.

When that happened, the Israelites had to pay 50 shekels of silver to redeem a man

> *"If your valuation is of a male from twenty years old up to sixty years old, then your valuation shall be fifty shekels of silver, according to the shekel of the sanctuary. If it is a female, then your valuation shall be thirty shekels; and if from five years old up to twenty years old, then your valuation for a male shall be twenty shekels."*
>
> LEVITICUS 27:3–5 NKJV

and 30 shekels to redeem a woman. Men were not worth more than women in ancient times just because they were male. The reason was simple: Men were physically stronger than women and could do more work; thus, they could earn more money in their lifetime than most women.

1998

Over 60 years of age, men were less able to do the hard, physical work in the fields, so it cost less to redeem them than a younger man or a woman. The Israelites still had to pay 30 shekels to redeem a 60-year-old woman, but that was *twice* as much as the 15 shekels needed to redeem a 61-year-old man.

In the United States, women have worked to obtain "equal rights" with men—including the right to vote. This postage stamp celebrates the 19th Amendment to the U.S. Constitution in 1920, granting women "suffrage."

And the LORD spake unto Moses in the wilderness of Sinai, in the tabernacle of the congregation, on the first day of the second month, in the second year after they were come out of the land of Egypt, saying, Take ye the sum of all the congregation of the children of Israel, after their families, by the house of their fathers, with the number of their names, every male by their polls. . . .
NUMBERS 1:1–2 KJV

The Bible's book of Numbers is about a "census"—a count of a nation's people. In the United States, that happens every ten years, in years ending in zero.

WHY DID GOD TELL MOSES TO COUNT ONLY THE MEN WHO CAME OUT OF EGYPT?

Two years after the children of Israel came out of Egypt, God told Moses to count every male "from twenty years old and above—all who are able to go to war" (Numbers 1:3 NKJV). The Israelites were about to invade the land of Canaan, so it was important to know how many fighting men they had. Because women and children wouldn't be going out to battle, they weren't counted. Even young men 18–19 years of age weren't counted.

Unfortunately, the Israelites were afraid to enter Canaan (Numbers 13–14), so God made them wander for 40 years in the wilderness until all the older generation who had been counted died. At the end of 40 years, when they had a whole new army ready to enter the Promised Land, God told Moses to conduct a second count of the fighting men (Numbers 26).

WHAT IS A NAZIRITE?

Priests and Levites were Israelites who were dedicated to the Lord their entire lives; they were set apart from the regular Israelites to serve God. But sometimes ordinary Israelites could also be dedicated to the Lord—either for their entire lives or for a short time. If a man or a woman felt that they should take some time to serve God, or to become closer to God, they could take a vow (promise) to become a Nazirite.

For as long as their vows lasted, they could not cut their hair, drink wine or vinegar or eat grapes, or come near a dead body (Numbers 6:1–8). Samson was a Nazirite his entire life (Judges 13:3–5).

The LORD said to Moses, "Speak to the Israelites and say to them: 'If a man or woman wants to make a special vow, a vow of dedication to the LORD as a Nazirite, they must abstain from wine and other fermented drink and must not drink vinegar made from wine or other fermented drink. They must not drink grape juice or eat grapes or raisins. As long as they remain under their Nazirite vow, they must not eat anything that comes from the grapevine, not even the seeds or skins. During the entire period of the Nazirite's vow, no razor may be used on their head. They must be holy until the period of their dedication to the LORD is over; they must let their hair grow long. Throughout the period of their dedication to the LORD, the Nazirite must not go near a dead body. Even if their own father or mother or brother or sister dies, they must not make themselves ceremonially unclean on account of them, because the symbol of their dedication to God is on their head. Throughout the period of their dedication, they are consecrated to the LORD.'"

NUMBERS 6:1–8 RSV

A long-haired lion is no match for the long-haired Samson, in this engraving from the 1800s. As a Nazirite, Samson was never supposed to cut his hair. When his enemies learned about that, they gave him a buzz cut— with disastrous results for Samson.

WHY DIDN'T GOD ALLOW MOSES TO ENTER THE PROMISED LAND JUST BECAUSE MOSES LOST HIS TEMPER ONE TIME?

When the Israelites were wandering thirsty in the desert, God told Moses to strike a rock with his staff and water would come out of it. Moses obeyed, and water gushed out (Exodus 17:1–7). Forty years later, the Israelites again needed water and complained. This time God commanded Moses to simply *speak* to a rock and water would flow out.

But Moses was angry at the people for complaining, and he shouted, "Hear now, you rebels! Must we bring water for you out of this rock?" (Numbers 20:10 NKJV). On top of it, he didn't believe that just speaking to the rock would work. So he hit it with his staff. No water came out. He hit it again. This time water gushed out.

> But the LORD said to Moses and Aaron, "Because you did not trust in me enough to honor me as holy in the sight of the Israelites, you will not bring this community into the land I give them."
>
> NUMBERS 20:12 TNIV

God did the miracle, but Moses had lacked faith and had lost his temper (Psalm 106:32–33). God said that because Moses didn't believe Him and didn't show proper respect to Him in front of the Israelites, Moses couldn't lead the people into the Promised Land (Deuteronomy 3:23–27).

Moses had a view like this of the Promised Land, from atop Mount Nebo. But his disobedience to God kept him from ever stepping into the land.

HOW WAS BALAAM'S DONKEY ABLE TO TALK?

> Then the LORD opened the donkey's mouth, and she said to Balaam, "What have I done to you to make you beat me these three times?"
>
> NUMBERS 22:28 NIV

Normally, animals, including donkeys, can't talk. That's why they're called dumb beasts. (*Dumb* means "unable to speak.") God didn't design a donkey's vocal cords to speak human language; they can barely make donkey sounds. Obviously,

He looks like he's talking—but this four-year-old donkey is only hee-hawing. God allowed a donkey to speak to a man named Balaam, scolding him for being so foolish!

God did a miracle to enable Balaam's donkey to speak.

Some people doubt that God could have done such a miracle. The funny thing is, if Balaam had had a parrot and the parrot had started speaking, no one would have been surprised. After all, in modern times, a parakeet named Puck had a vocabulary of 1,728 words, and Bibi, a Congo African gray parrot, can speak 20 languages. Clearly, God designed their brains and vocal cords for speaking. You can hardly get them to keep quiet.

God did an astonishing miracle to allow Balaam's donkey to speak intelligently in human language.

WHAT ARE "HIGH PLACES," AND WHAT WAS SO BAD ABOUT THEM?........⊃

When the Israelites prepared to drive out the Canaanites, God ordered, "Destroy all their carved images and their. . .idols, and demolish all their high places" (Numbers 33:52 NIV). The Israelites had to destroy the idols of the Canaanite gods Baal and Asherah because these gods were actually demons (1 Corinthians 10:19–20). If they left the idols standing, the Israelites might be tempted to worship them (Exodus 23:32–33).

"Drive out all the inhabitants of the land before you. Destroy all their carved images and their cast idols, and demolish all their high places."

NUMBERS 33:52 NIV

The Canaanites often worshipped on top of mountains and hills, the "high places" where they felt closer to their gods. That's where the altars to their demon-gods were located, and that's where the Canaanites did their disgusting worship. So God told the Israelites to tear apart the Canaanite altars on the high places.

God wanted His people to have nothing to do with these defiled "high places." He wanted His people to worship Him at the temple on Mount Zion—the mountain He chose—not on whatever high place they chose themselves (Deuteronomy 12:2–14).

⊃ **Jerusalem was the only "high place" where God wanted His people to worship.**

And he humbled thee, and suffered thee to hunger, and fed thee with manna, which thou knewest not, neither did thy fathers know; that he might make thee know that man doth not live by bread only, but by every word that proceedeth out of the mouth of the LORD doth man live. Thy raiment waxed not old upon thee, neither did thy foot swell, these forty years.
DEUTORONOMY 8:3–4 KJV

HOW DID THE ISRAELITES SURVIVE IN THE DESERT FOR 40 YEARS?

A few shepherds still live in the Sinai Desert today, and they scrounge around and find enough food and water, as well as pasture for their flocks. But there were so *many* Israelites—perhaps a couple of million—that there simply wasn't enough food for all of them to eat. God had to do huge miracles to supply them with food.

For example, for 40 years, He caused a delicious, nutritional food called manna to come down from heaven. He also sent vast flocks of quail flying into their camp—twice (Exodus 16; Numbers 11:4–9, 31–32)! God also did miracles to give them water to drink (Exodus 15:22–25; 17:1–7; Numbers 20:1–13).

God even did miracles to keep their feet from swelling with all their wandering in the desert, and kept their clothing from wearing out for 40 years (Deuteronomy 8:4). God did countless miracles to help His people survive. He had to, or they wouldn't have made it.

It would be hard to spend forty minutes—let alone forty years—in a place like the Sinai Desert. But God performed miracles to keep His people alive in the desert for four decades.

HOW DID THE ISRAELITES KEEP FROM GETTING SICK WHEN THEY KNEW NOTHING ABOUT GERMS AND DISEASE?......................

God knows everything there is to know about germs. However, if He had explained to the Israelites what causes sickness, they still wouldn't have understood. So God simply gave them practical rules to prevent them from getting sick in the first place.

For example, being careless with human waste is a major cause of a disease called dysentery, so God ordered the Israelites to keep their toilets away from their camps (Deuteronomy 23:12–14).

As recently as 200 years ago, most people didn't know enough to wash the germs off their hands, yet the Jews have been thoroughly washing their hands for thousands of years, in keeping with God's commands (Mark 7:3–4).

God also told the Israelites to quarantine anyone who had an infectious skin disease, and He explained how to get rid of mildew that caused asthma and other health problems (Leviticus 13; 14:33–57).

Aliens from outer space? No—the "swine flu" virus, magnified thousands of times. Many of God's rules for His people in the Old Testament were to protect them from sicknesses carried by germs and viruses like this.

Designate a place outside the camp where you can go to relieve yourself. As part of your equipment have something to dig with, and when you relieve yourself, dig a hole and cover up your excrement. For the LORD your God moves about in your camp to protect you and to deliver your enemies to you. Your camp must be holy, so that he will not see among you anything indecent and turn away from you.

DEUTERONOMY 23:12–14 TNIV

ARE CHRISTIANS TODAY SUPPOSED TO TITHE?

Different churches have different opinions about tithing. In Old Testament times, God commanded the Israelites to give 10 percent of all their earnings and flocks and crops to Him. This tithe was used to support the Levites and priests in the temple, and also provided food for the poor and the widows and orphans. God promised to bless and protect the Israelites if they tithed (Malachi 3:8–12). That was the law in Old Testament times.

Many churches believe that Christians today are also supposed to tithe; they say that most financial problems are caused by people failing to give one-tenth of their income to God.

Other churches point out that the New Testament doesn't tell Christians to tithe. However, Jesus did talk a lot about giving generously (Luke 6:38), and the apostle Paul urged believers to give as much as they were able (2 Corinthians 9:6–8). Whether you believe in tithing or not, part of being a Christian is giving to God and others.

> Every third year, the year of the tithe, give a tenth of your produce to the Levite, the foreigner, the orphan, and the widow so that they may eat their fill in your cities. And then, in the Presence of GOD, your God, say this: I have brought the sacred share, I've given it to the Levite, foreigner, orphan, and widow. What you commanded, I've done. I haven't detoured around your commands, I haven't forgotten a single one.
>
> DEUTERONOMY 26:12–13 MSG

"God Loves a cheerful giver" is what the Bible says (2 Corinthians 9:7). He doesn't need the money—but He knows it's good for us not to be too attached to the stuff!

37

WHY WAS CANAAN CALLED THE PROMISED LAND?

"You shall give this people possession of the land which I swore to their fathers to give them."
JOSHUA 1:6 NASB

God promised Abraham that He would give the land of Canaan to him and to his descendants. In fact, God promised him the land again and again (Genesis 12:7; 13:14–17; 15:7; 17:8). God later made the same promise to Abraham's son Isaac (Genesis 26:2–4) and to Isaac's son Jacob (Genesis 28:13–14). No wonder Canaan was called the Promised Land.

When the older generation of Israelites were fearful and doubted that God could bring them into the land He had promised them, God let them all die in the wilderness. He then promised that, 40 years later, when their children were grown up, He would bring the younger generation into Canaan (Numbers 14:26–31). God declared that Joshua would be the one to lead the children of Israel into the Promised Land (Joshua 1:5–6). And he did!

Boundaries of the Promised Land

WHY DID GOD BLESS RAHAB THE PROSTITUTE EVEN THOUGH SHE TOLD A LIE?

But the woman had taken the two men and hidden them; and she said, "True, men came to me, but I did not know where they came from; and when the gate was to be closed, at dark, the men went out; where the men went I do not know; pursue them quickly, for you will overtake them." But she had brought them up to the roof, and hid them with the stalks of flax which she had laid in order on the roof.

JOSHUA 2:4–6 RSV

The Bible tells us, "Do not lie. Do not deceive one another" (Leviticus 19:11 NIV). Yet we also know that undercover police officers must pretend to be someone else to bring criminals to justice. They can't tell the truth about who they are, what they're doing, or where they're going. Also, when our country is at war, brave men and women who serve as spies must use deception. Citizens of enemy nations who help them must conceal the truth also.

Israel was at war with the nations that lived in Canaan, so the two Israelite spies tried to make the people of Jericho think they were ordinary travelers. Somehow their cover was blown, and when Rahab realized that, she hid them on her roof. Aiding the enemy was a crime for a loyal citizen of Jericho, but Rahab now believed in God (Joshua 2:8–11) and had new loyalties. She was like a secret agent operating a safe house—so yes, she lied to protect the spies when their lives were in danger.

Remember the story of Pinnochio, the wooden toy that came to life—but whose nose grew every time he told a lie? This drawing is from an early edition of the Pinnochio story.

For protecting God's people, Rahab and her family were spared and she was allowed to live in Israel the rest of her life (Joshua 6:25). Many Christians believe she was an ancestor of Jesus (Matthew 1:5).

HOW DID THE JORDAN RIVER PART?

"And as soon as the priests who carry the ark of the LORD—the Lord of all the earth—set foot in the Jordan, its waters flowing downstream will be cut off and stand up in a heap."

JOSHUA 3:13 TNIV

Normally, the Jordan River near Jericho is not wide, but it was springtime and the river was swollen with rain and melted snow. It overflowed its banks, filled the flood plains, and was nearly a mile wide. But as soon as the priests stepped into the river carrying the ark of the covenant, the water level fell until the riverbed was empty. Only after all the Israelites had crossed

The Jordan isn't normally a huge river. . .but when the Israelites crossed, it was at flood stage. But that's no match for a miracle-working God.

through did the river start flowing again.

How did God achieve this miracle? Well, "the waters which came down from upstream stood still, and rose in a heap very far away at Adam" (Joshua 3:16 NKJV). Adam was a town 20 miles upstream from Jericho. The river gorge is narrow there, and sometimes the cliffs collapse and a landslide dams the river. This happened in 1927, blocking the Jordan River for 20 hours.

How did God cause the landslide in Joshua's day? It could have been the heavy spring rains. Or, very likely, God sent an earthquake to shake the hills (Psalm 114:3–7). Even if God used natural means, the *exact timing* of the river drying up was a huge miracle. And speaking of timing, as soon as the last Israelite walked out of the riverbed, the Jordan flooded back again.

HOW DID THE WALLS OF JERICHO FALL DOWN?

Jericho was the first city the Israelites came to when they entered Canaan. God could have simply allowed them to besiege it, but He wanted the Canaanites to fear His mighty power. He therefore had Joshua's army march silently around the city once a day for six days while the priests blew trumpets. On the seventh day, the army marched around Jericho seven times. When the priests gave a long blast on the trumpets, the entire army shouted and the city walls collapsed (Joshua 6).

When the trumpets sounded, the people shouted, and at the sound of the trumpet, when the people gave a loud shout, the wall collapsed; so every man charged straight in, and they took the city.

JOSHUA 6:20 NIV

How did this happen? Bible scholar Kenneth Kitchen believes that there may have been an earthquake at the precise moment that the Israelites shouted, and this brought the walls down. God sometimes sent earthquakes as a sign of His power (Isaiah 29:6; Ezekiel 38:18–20; Matthew 27:50–54; 28:2).

Some people guess that the shouting and the trumpet blast vibrated the walls and caused them to collapse, but that's not likely. Otherwise the Israelites would have done that to *every* Canaanite city.

The city of Ávila, in central Spain, is surrounded by walls just like the biblical Jericho was. Ávila's walls were built nearly a thousand years ago!

WHY DID GOD TELL THE ISRAELITES TO KILL THE CANAANITES—MEN, WOMEN, AND CHILDREN? WASN'T THAT TOTALLY CRUEL?

They put everything in the city under the holy curse, killing man and woman, young and old, ox and sheep and donkey.

JOSHUA 6:21 MSG

Canaanite society was so corrupt that God said that He was casting them out to make room for the Israelites; in fact, the Canaanites were so wicked that the land itself was *vomiting* them out (Leviticus 18:24–25).

God tried to strike such fear into the Canaanites that those who weren't totally corrupted would fear His power and flee the land. That's why He did such astonishing miracles—and the Canaanites did indeed fear God. Rahab told the spies, "Our hearts melted and no courage remained in any man" (Joshua 2:11 NASB).

God told the Israelites again and again to "drive them out" (Exodus 23:27–31; 34:11; Deuteronomy 7:1). The Canaanites simply could have fled south to Egypt. In the past, tens of thousands of Canaanites had migrated to Egypt—and at that time there was a huge need for workers because a couple of million Israelite slaves had moved out.

Sad to say, the evil Canaanites hardened their hearts and stayed—even though they knew that God Himself was fighting them; even though they knew that the Israelites were prepared to wipe them out (Joshua 9:24; 10:1–5). The Canaanites who dug in their heels to fight God brought destruction on themselves and their families.

DID THE SUN ACTUALLY STAND STILL WHEN JOSHUA PRAYED THAT IT WOULD?

One day, five Amorite kings surrounded the Israelites' allies at Gibeon, so the Israelites attacked the Amorites. Joshua wanted to finish the battle before sunset, so he prayed, "Sun, stand still over Gibeon." The Bible says, "The sun stood still in the middle of the sky and did not go down for a whole day" (Joshua 10:12–13 GNT).

Then Joshua spoke to the LORD in the day when the LORD delivered up the Amorites before the sons of Israel, and he said in the sight of Israel, "O sun, stand still at Gibeon, and O moon in the valley of Aijalon." So the sun stood still, and the moon stopped, until the nation avenged themselves of their enemies.

JOSHUA 10:12–13 NASB

We know that the sun doesn't move around the earth, but that the earth's rotation makes the sun appear to rise and set. So did the earth abruptly stop rotating? No. That would have caused global destruction, wiping out the Israelites, too. Perhaps God refracted the sun's light so that it appeared as if it were staying in the same spot for the rest of the day.

This story comes from the lost book of Jashar,

which describes the Israelites' wars in poetry. (See Joshua 10:13; 2 Samuel 1:18.) Some of the poetry is symbolic, such as when it describes Israel's rulers as "swifter than eagles" (2 Samuel 1:23), though, of course, no one can actually run 200 miles per hour.

We know that God did a miracle that day, but exactly what kind of miracle is a mystery.

Joshua asks God to stop the sun, in an 1816 painting by John Martin.

WHY WERE THERE SO MANY WARS AND KILLINGS IN THE OLD TESTAMENT? WHY DIDN'T THE ISRAELITES JUST LOVE THEIR ENEMIES LIKE JESUS SAID?.................

Jesus said, "Love your enemies" (Matthew 5:44 NIV), and "If someone strikes you on the right cheek, turn to him the other also" (Matthew 5:39 NIV). This may mean avoiding a fight by letting someone insult you or slap you. But there comes a point when even Christians have to use physical force to stop someone from beating them up or to defend their loved ones.

Joshua waged war against all these kings for a long time. Except for the Hitites living in Gibeon, not one city made a treaty of peace with the Israelites, who took them all in battle.

JOSHUA 11:18–19 TNIV

The apostle Paul said that the police and armed forces do not "bear the sword" for no reason. They are appointed by God Himself to "execute wrath on him who practices evil" (Romans 13:4 NKJV). So when an enemy nation attacks, it is the duty of Christian soldiers to use their weapons to defend their country.

Wars have been fought throughout human history, and since the days of the New Testament, Christians have had to fight. Sometimes wars can be avoided, but often they cannot.

WHO WAS BAAL, AND WHY DID THE ISRAELITES WORSHIP HIM?

Then the Israelites did evil in the eyes of the Lord and served the Baals.
JUDGES 2:11 NIV

Canaan was a dry land that depended on rain to produce crops. The Canaanites had many gods, but they worshipped Baal most of all because they believed he controlled the weather and the rain. The Canaanites also thought Baal was the fertility god, who caused animals to bear their young and who blessed people with children. They gave Baal credit for everything that *God* was really doing.

As if that weren't bad enough, when people worshipped Baal, they cut themselves, ate unclean animals, and slept with prostitutes (1 Kings 18:28; Isaiah 65:2–4).

God had forbidden people to make idols of *Him*, yet there were often idols of Baal around. When the land went through a dry spell, the people were tempted to bow down to the idol of Baal, hoping that it could bring rain.

This figurine of Baal is more than 3,000 years old!

43

WHY DID GOD DO SUCH HUGE MIRACLES IN OLDEN DAYS BUT DOESN'T DO THEM TODAY?......

Gideon asked that very question nearly 3,500 years ago! When Israel was overrun by invaders, Gideon asked why God wasn't doing mighty miracles to rescue Israel as He had done many years earlier—such as when He sent plagues on Egypt and parted the Red Sea. Gideon knew that God still *could* do miracles if He chose to, but he complained that the Lord had abandoned them (Judges 6:13).

Gideon was partially right. A prophet had just finished telling Israel that because they had disobeyed and abandoned God, God was allowing them to suffer (Judges 6:7–10). But when they learned their lesson and turned back to God, He chose Gideon to lead Israel's armies and did miracles to deliver them.

> *Then Gideon said, "Sir, if the Lord is with us, why are we having so much trouble? Where are the miracles our ancestors told us he did when the Lord brought them out of Egypt? But now he has left us and handed us over to the Midianites."*
>
> JUDGES 6:13 NCV

Some people say the birth of a baby is a miracle—and though it is an amazing thing, it happens millions of times each year, all around the world. True miracles are really unusual, like when Moses parted the Red Sea or the walls of Jericho fell before the people of Israel.

At first Gideon had trouble believing that God could use him to rescue His people. Doubt is another reason why God sometimes doesn't do miracles. When Jesus returned to His hometown of Nazareth, the Bible says, "He did not do many mighty works there, because of their unbelief" (Matthew 13:58 RSV). We have to believe God (Mark 9:23).

IF GIDEON WAS SO FEARFUL AND DOUBTING, HOW DID HE BECOME SUCH A GREAT HERO?

> *"Pardon me, my lord," Gideon replied, "but how can I save Israel? My clan is the weakest in Manasseh, and I am the least in my family."*
>
> JUDGES 6:15 NIV

When an angel declared that God was going to use Gideon to rescue Israel, Gideon believed him but still had doubts. Nevertheless, he trusted God enough to obey. Even though he was afraid, he destroyed his father's idols. He then gathered an army and prepared for battle. Then Gideon got cold feet, so he asked God to do two small miracles to show that He was really with him. God did the miracles, and Gideon was reassured.

Gideon was facing a monster-sized army and had only 32,000 men—yet God told him to send almost his entire army home. What a test! Yet Gideon believed and obeyed. God then told Gideon that he would save Israel with only three hundred men. Gideon obeyed. God knew that Gideon was afraid, so to encourage him, God let him overhear an amazing dream. God then gave Gideon a crazy, wild battle plan—and it worked!

All of this should encourage us. Even though we struggle with fears and doubts, God can use us to do great things as long as we trust and obey Him.

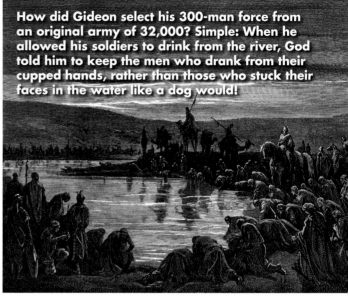

How did Gideon select his 300-man force from an original army of 32,000? Simple: When he allowed his soldiers to drink from the river, God told him to keep the men who drank from their cupped hands, rather than those who stuck their faces in the water like a dog would!

WHY DID JEPHTHAH HAVE TO KEEP HIS VOW TO SACRIFICE HIS DAUGHTER?........→

One time the Israelites chose a bandit chief named Jephthah to liberate them from their oppressors. As he marched out to battle, Jephthah vowed to the Lord that if God helped him win, when he returned home, he would sacrifice to God whatever came out of the door of his house to greet him.

Jephthah was shocked when his only child, a daughter, came out the door—but what was he *hoping* would step out first? His wife? A servant? His dog? The family's goat? It was a very thoughtless vow to make.

Maybe Jephthah expected an animal to greet him at his front door. But whatever the case, his vow was a foolish one.

Alas, my daughter! thou hast brought me very low, and thou art one of them that trouble me: for I have opened my mouth unto the LORD, and I cannot go back. And she said unto him, My father, if thou hast opened thy mouth unto the LORD, do to me according to that which hath proceeded out of thy mouth.

JUDGES 11:35–36 KJV

Jephthah knew that men were supposed to keep vows they made; otherwise they would be "guilty of sin" (Deuteronomy 23:21 NIV). So he sacrificed his daughter. But by doing so, he committed a much greater sin. When the Israelites foolishly sacrificed their sons and daughters, God called it a terrible sin and said, "I never commanded, nor did it enter my mind, that they should do such a detestable thing" (Jeremiah 32:35 NIV).

WHY DID SAMSON LOSE ALL HiS STRENGTH JUST BECAUSE OF A HAIRCUT?......... →

When Delilah cut Samson's hair, he lost his supernatural strength and became as weak as any other man. But remember: Samson's great strength was not actually in his hair. It was a gift from God (Judges 14:6; 15:14), which he lost when "the LORD had departed from him" (Judges 16:20 NKJV).

The reason it was important that Samson's hair never be cut was because he was a Nazirite—someone specially dedicated to God. Among other things, Nazirites were not allowed to cut their hair (Judges 13:4–5). When Samson told Delilah that cutting his hair would make him lose his strength, he knew good and well that she would try to do it. (After all, the previous three times he told her something that would make him lose his strength, she had done precisely what he said.)

> Does Samson's story teach us that haircuts are bad? No. . .Samson got in trouble with God for breaking his promise, not just for cutting his hair.

By telling Delilah to cut his hair, Samson broke the rules of a Nazirite. Once Samson was no longer dedicated to the Lord, God departed from him and removed the gift of strength.

> She kept at it day after day, nagging and tormenting him. Finally, he was fed up—he couldn't take another minute of it. He spilled it. He told her, "A razor has never touched my head. I've been God's Nazirite from conception. If I were shaved, my strength would leave me; I would be as helpless as any other mortal." When Delilah realized that he had told her his secret, she sent for the Philistine tyrants, telling them, "Come quickly—this time he's told me the truth." They came, bringing the bribe money. When she got him to sleep, his head on her lap, she motioned to a man to cut off the seven braids of his hair. Immediately he began to grow weak. His strength drained from him. Then she said, "The Philistines are on you, Samson!" He woke up, thinking, "I'll go out, like always, and shake free." He didn't realize that GOD had abandoned him.
>
> JUDGES 16:17–20 MSG

"Blessed are you of the Lord, my daughter! For you have shown more kindness at the end than at the beginning, in that you did not go after young men, whether poor or rich."
RUTH 3:10 NKJV

"Marrying for the money"?
Some people do, but that
wasn't Ruth's style.

WAS RUTH CONNIVING AND GREEDY FOR GOING AFTER A RICH, OLDER MAN?

Once in a while, you hear about a young woman marrying a rich, older man, and people say, "She just married him for his money!" Some women do that, but that is not what Ruth did—even though she followed Naomi's advice and offered herself in marriage to a wealthy, older man.

Ruth was a deeply spiritual widow from Moab, who had forsaken her family, her country, and her pagan gods to follow her mother-in-law, Naomi, back to Israel. Ruth knew that Naomi was desperately poor and had nothing to offer her, but she went with Naomi because she loved God and wanted to serve Him, and she loved Naomi and wanted to take care of her. Those two things are what made Boaz admire Ruth (Ruth 1:16–17; 2:10–12).

WHAT IS A KINSMAN REDEEMER?.....→

Family was very important in ancient Israel, and brothers and sisters and close relatives looked out for one another. It was a law, in fact, that if a man became very poor and had to sell his land, his closest relative (kinsman) was to come and buy back (redeem) the land that the poor man had sold (Leviticus 25:25). That way the land stayed in the family. The relative who did this was called the kinsman redeemer. If the closest relative couldn't afford to buy the land—or refused to—then the responsibility passed to the next nearest relative.

A man named Elimelech had sold his land during a famine, and when his widow, Naomi, came back years later, she had no land and no money to buy it back. A kinsman said he would redeem her land, but Boaz reminded the man that when he bought the land, he also had to marry Ruth, the widow of Naomi's son. That was also according to the law. The relative then said that he couldn't redeem the land. Boaz then became the kinsman redeemer (Ruth 4).

> "Although it is true that I am near of kin, there is a kinsman-redeemer nearer than I."
> RUTH 3:12 NIV

A giant statue called Christ the Redeemer towers over Rio de Janeiro, Brazil. Boaz, by "buying back" Ruth, was an example of what Jesus would later do for everyone who believes in Him.

WHY WAS IT SO IMPORTANT IN OLD TESTAMENT DAYS TO HAVE CHILDREN?

> "May your house be like the house of Perez, whom Tamar bore to Judah, because of the children that the LORD will give you by this young woman."
> RUTH 4:12 RSV

In ancient Israel, as in the early days of America, there were several reasons why it was important for a husband and wife to have children—*several* children. First of all, there was always lots of work to do on the family farm, and the more sons and daughters there were, the more work could get done.

Second, parents cared for their children and provided for them when they were young, and it was expected that when the parents became old, their grown children would then care for them. The more children a couple had, the more certain it was that they would be cared for in their old age, and the more they felt blessed by God. Therefore, they looked forward to having seven or even ten sons (Psalm 127:3–5; Ruth 4:15; 1 Samuel 1:8).

A Dutch artist portrayed Hannah presenting her baby, Samuel, to Eli the priest, in 1665.

And she made a vow, saying, "O LORD Almighty, if you will only look upon your servant's misery and remember me, and not forget your servant but give her a son, then I will give him to the LORD for all the days of his life, and no razor will ever be used on his head."

1 SAMUEL 1:11 NIV

WHERE DID THE PRACTICE OF DEDICATING CHILDREN COME FROM?

Many churches have ceremonies in which parents bring their newborn baby to the front of the church to have a pastor pray over him or her. The parents promise to raise their child to serve God. This is called a baby dedication or dedicating a child to the Lord.

The practice is based on the story of Samuel. His mother, Hannah, couldn't have children, so she promised God that if He gave her a son, she would give him back to the Lord. Sure enough, she had a son, named Samuel, and when he was about three years old, she brought him to God's temple and gave him into the care of Eli the priest. Samuel grew up serving God there, and his mother visited him once a year (1 Samuel 1:24–28; 2:18–19). Samuel became a great man of God.

Today after parents "give their children to God," they raise them at home and teach them to dedicate their hearts and lives to God.

IF THE ARK OF THE COVENANT WAS SO SPECIAL, WHY DID GOD ALLOW THE PHILISTINES TO CAPTURE IT?.......

Here's the ark of the covenant, Hollywood-style, from the 1981 film *Raiders of the Lost Ark*. Nobody knows where the ark went after the Babylonians destroyed Jerusalem in 586 BC.

God didn't dwell in the ark, but He sometimes appeared there (Exodus 25:22). The Israelites, however, began to believe that God was *always* there, even when they disobeyed Him—and at this time they were very disobedient.

> So the Philistines fought, and Israel was defeated, and they fled, every man to his home; and there was a very great slaughter, for there fell of Israel thirty thousand foot soldiers. And the ark of God was captured.
>
> 1 SAMUEL 4:10–11 RSV

They thought that the ark itself would help them. They said, "Let us bring the ark of the covenant. . .that when it comes among us it may save us from the hand of our enemies" (1 Samuel 4:3 NKJV).

God taught the Israelites a very good lesson when He allowed the Philistines to capture the ark: They needed to obey *Him*—not just depend on the ark—if they wanted Him to be with them.

God also showed that He was more than able to protect the ark from the Philistines. He sent so many plagues on the Philistines that they willingly sent the ark back to Israel (1 Samuel 5–6).

WHY DID THE SONS OF SUCH A GODLY MAN AS SAMUEL TURN OUT BAD?

> When Samuel became old, he made his sons judges over Israel. The name of his first-born son was Jo'el, and the name of his second, Abi'jah; they were judges in Beer-sheba. Yet his sons did not walk in his ways, but turned aside after gain; they took bribes and perverted justice. Then all the elders of Israel gathered together and came to Samuel at Ramah, and said to him, "Behold, you are old and your sons do not walk in your ways; now appoint for us a king to govern us like all the nations."
>
> 1 SAMUEL 8:1–5 RSV

We all bear responsibility for our own actions, but sometimes when children turn out bad, it's partially the parents' fault. For example, Eli the high priest knew all about the terrible things his sons were doing, yet he didn't discipline them. He didn't take away their jobs as priests, even though their jobs gave them many opportunities to offend and hurt people (1 Samuel 2:12–17, 27–30; 3:13).

Sometimes, however, even when parents discipline their children and teach them the right way to live and set an example of honoring God, the children still choose to be disobedient. This is what happened with Samuel's sons. Unlike their father, they refused to walk with God (1 Samuel 8:1–5).

Every person is responsible for his or her own choices. Hezekiah was a godly king, yet his son Manasseh was an evil king. Then again, Manasseh's grandson Josiah truly loved God (2 Kings 18:1–7; 21:1–11; 22:1–2). No matter how good or how evil a king was, his sons made their own choices about whether to serve God.

"A wise son heeds his father's instruction," Proverbs 13:1 (NIV) says, "but a mocker does not listen to rebuke." And if a son (or daughter) ignores Dad's advice for too long, they might find themselves in this guy's situation!

KING SAUL WAS SUCH A GREAT LEADER IN THE BEGINNING. WHY DID HE END UP FAILING SO MISERABLY?

As a young man, Saul was tall and strong, yet he was very humble and shy. When he heard that he had been chosen as king, he hid himself (1 Samuel 9:2; 10:21–24). The Bible says that Saul was "small in his own eyes" (1 Samuel 15:17). Because he depended on God to help him, Saul was victorious in his battles with Israel's enemies (1 Samuel 11:6–11; 14:47–48).

But Saul had four weaknesses: He became impatient and fearful when God's prophet didn't show up on time; he began disobeying God's clear instructions; he valued the opinions of other people too much; and he became power hungry, insecure, and violent toward his competition (1 Samuel 13:1–13; 15:1–31; 18:1–12).

"You acted foolishly," Samuel said. "You have not kept the command the LORD your God gave you; if you had, he would have established your kingdom over Israel for all time. But now your kingdom will not endure; the LORD has sought out a man after his own heart and appointed him leader of his people, because you have not kept the LORD's command."

1 SAMUEL 13:13–14 NIV

Instead of seeking and obeying God, Saul allowed these weaknesses to take over his life and develop into major problems, and that is why he fell.

Like King Saul, Benedict Arnold was a military leader who fell into disgrace. A general in the Continental Army during the American Revolution, Arnold was angry that leaders in the colonies didn't seem to appreciate him—so he switched sides and joined the British. Benedict Arnold is now a name that means "traitor."

WHAT DID SAMUEL MEAN WHEN HE SAID, "OBEDIENCE IS BETTER THAN SACRIFICE"?........

An evil tribe of raiders called Amalekites lived in the desert south of Israel. They were like a band of criminals. They hated God and had been terrorizing Israel for hundreds of years, killing and robbing and enslaving God's people. God finally had enough and had Samuel give King Saul very clear orders: Saul was to wipe out the Amalekites—every single one—and kill all their herds and flocks as well.

Saul disobeyed God. First, he allowed many Amalekites to escape, so that David had to fight them later (1 Samuel 30). Saul also decided to spare the king of the Amalekites and bring him back as a trophy; and he didn't destroy the Amalekites' herds and flocks. He brought the fattest calves and the lambs back to Israel to sacrifice to God.

The Lord was *not* pleased with Saul's sacrifice. He wanted Saul simply to do what He had told him to do.

> Saul had other disobedience problems with Samuel—like the time Saul found a witch to call the dead Samuel's spirit. This painting, from the 1600s, shows Saul falling before a ghostly—and unhappy—Samuel. Read the whole story in 1 Samuel 28.

> ↓
> But Samuel replied: "Does the LORD delight in burnt offerings and sacrifices as much as in obeying the voice of the LORD? To obey is better than sacrifice, and to heed is better than the fat of rams."
>
> 1 SAMUEL 15:22 NIV

: WHAT MADE KING DAVID ISRAEL'S GREATEST LEADER?...

> → GOD said, "Up on your feet! Anoint him! This is the one."
>
> 1 SAMUEL 16:12 MSG

King Saul didn't love God wholeheartedly and disobeyed Him, so God rejected Saul as king. The prophet Samuel told Saul, "The LORD has sought out a man after his own heart" (1 Samuel 13:14 NIV). That man was David. This didn't mean that David was perfect or sinless. David made mistakes, too, but his heart was in the right place and he loved God intensely. When he sinned, he repented sincerely.

The apostle Paul shed more light on this when he quoted God, saying, "I have found David son of Jesse a man after my own heart; he will do everything I want him to do" (Acts 13:22 NIV). Saul constantly disobeyed and did very little of what God wanted him to do. David loved God and did everything God wanted him to do. Because of David's love and obedience, God made him Israel's greatest leader.

Four of the United States' greatest leaders—George Washington, Thomas Jefferson, Theodore Roosevelt, and Abraham Lincoln—are carved into the side of a rock hill in South Dakota. The presidents honored at Mount Rushmore were wise and strong leaders like the Bible's King David. But it was David's obedience to God that made him Israel's greatest leader.

WHAT DOES IT MEAN TO BE ANOINTED?....

To "anoint" means to pour or spread oil on someone. There were three main reasons in the Bible for doing this:

> Then Samuel took the horn of oil, and anointed him in the midst of his brethren.
>
> 1 SAMUEL 16:13 KJV

1. People anointed themselves with perfume by spreading perfumed or scented oils on their bodies (Ruth 3:3; Esther 2:12). They also spread oil on their skin to make their faces shiny (Psalm 104:15).

2. Olive oil was poured on the heads of priests, prophets, and kings to dedicate them to God (Exodus 28:41; 1 Samuel 16:1, 13). The oil symbolized the presence of the Holy Spirit, who would then help the person.

3. In the New Testament, Christians anointed sick people with oil when praying for them to be healed (James 5:14).

WHY DID DAVID TAKE FIVE STONES WHEN HE WENT TO FIGHT GOLIATH, WHEN HE ONLY NEEDED ONE TO KILL HIM?..............

> Then he took his staff in his hand, chose five smooth stones from the stream, put them in the pouch of his shepherd's bag and, with his sling in his hand, approached the Philistine.
>
> 1 SAMUEL 17:40 NIV

David was a good shot with the sling, but Goliath was covered with armor. He had a bronze helmet on his head and wore a coat of scale armor weighing 125 pounds. He even wore bronze shin guards. Another Philistine, carrying a shield, walked in front of Goliath (1 Samuel 17:4–7). David knew that he had to hit Goliath in the face, but there was no guarantee the stone would kill the giant; it might only wound him. Besides, there was the shield bearer to consider.

When David's first stone embedded in Goliath's forehead, the shield bearer apparently dropped the shield and ran. David ran up and found that the rock had killed the giant (1 Samuel 17:50–51). As it turned out, David didn't need the four extra stones, but he figured it would be wise to take them as a backup, just in case.

David's sling probably looked something like this. He would whirl it around and around until the stone inside the pouch had gained enough speed, then release one end of the string to let the rock fly. And David's first rock found its way right into Goliath's head!

WHY DID DAVID FIGHT SO MANY WARS?

David didn't *want* to fight all those wars. In almost every case, an enemy provoked him and David was forced to fight. After Saul died, David was God's choice as king, but one of Saul's generals declared Saul's son Ishbosheth to be king and fought against David. David finally united the kingdom of Israel peacefully (2 Samuel 2:1–9; 5:1–3).

Then the Philistines invaded Israel, but David defeated them (2 Samuel 5:17–25). Then the Ammonites disgraced David's ambassadors, and when they realized that they had started a war, they hired the Arameans to help crush David's armies—but David defeated them all (2 Samuel 8, 10). In later years, David's son Absalom led an army against him, and an Israelite named Sheba started a civil war, but David fought back and defeated them both (2 Samuel 15–20).

King David is known as a mighty warrior—and he was—but he was usually forced into that role. When you read the Psalms, you will see again and again that David prayed for God to protect him from his enemies who were plotting against him.

Now after this it came about that David defeated the Philistines and subdued them. . . .
2 SAMUEL 8:1 NASB

The weapons have changed over the years, but humans have been fighting wars almost since the beginning of history.

HOW DID DAVID GET AWAY WITH STEALING ANOTHER MAN'S WIFE AND KILLING THE MAN?...

Uriah, kneeling, takes a letter from King David, in a painting from the 1400s. Uriah delivered the secret message—which called for his own death!

David did *not* get away with those things. The Bible tells us that David committed adultery with Bathsheba while her husband, Uriah, was away at war. When Bathsheba became pregnant and David couldn't cover his sin, he had Uriah sent into the heaviest fighting; then the rest of the army was ordered to retreat, leaving Uriah alone to die.

> David had her brought to his house, and she became his wife and bore him a son. But the thing David had done displeased the LORD.
>
> 2 SAMUEL 11:27 TNIV

When God sent a prophet to confront the king about the terrible things he had done, David realized that God would have been justified to kill him for his crimes. You can read David's prayer of repentance in Psalm 51. God forgave David and said that he wouldn't die.

Nevertheless, God punished David by allowing Bathsheba's child to become sick and die. God also allowed David's adult son Absalom to wage war against him and to sleep with David's wives (2 Samuel 12:11–19).

WHY DID ABSALOM REBEL AGAINST HIS FATHER, KING DAVID, AND TRY TO BECOME KING IN HIS PLACE?....

David's handsome son Absalom gets his beautiful long hair caught in a tree branch—and soon loses his life.

Absalom had two reasons. First, he despised his father for not doing justice when David's son Amnon raped Absalom's sister. David *was* furious with Amnon, but Absalom thought David didn't punish him enough—so he took the law into his own hands and murdered Amnon (2 Samuel 13).

David eventually forgave Absalom, but soon Absalom was telling every Israelite

> Absalom sent secret messengers throughout all the tribes of Israel, saying, "As soon as you hear the sound of the trumpet, then say, 'Absalom is king at Hebron!'"
>
> 2 SAMUEL 15:10 RSV

that David hadn't done what was right. Absalom said that if *he* were king, he would do justice (2 Samuel 15:1–6). Becoming king would mean murdering his own father and raping his father's wives, but Absalom didn't see anything unjust about that.

Second, Absalom was so handsome that everyone in Israel praised him. In fact, Absalom was in love with himself and was convinced that he was so royally good-looking that he surely ought to be king. He was especially proud of his long, pretty hair (2 Samuel 14:25–26), which eventually became his downfall.

WHY WAS IT SUCH A SIN FOR DAVID TO COUNT HOW MANY SOLDIERS HE HAD IN HIS ARMY?

> "Go about now through all the tribes of Israel, from Dan to Beersheba, and register the people, that I may know the number of the people."
>
> 2 SAMUEL 24:2 NASB

God didn't have a problem with the rulers of Israel counting how many fighting men they had. After all, in the past, God Himself had *twice* ordered Moses to conduct a census (Numbers 1:1–2; 26:1–2).

However, the Bible makes it clear that Satan was the one who inspired David to do this particular census, and God allowed it because God was upset with Israel for their disobedience (2 Samuel 24:1; 1 Chronicles 21:1). Why did David listen to the devil? Satan probably appealed to David's pride. After all, David had just finished conquering a huge empire that stretched from Egypt in the south to the Euphrates River in the north.

"Some trust in chariots and some in horses," David wrote in Psalm 20:7 (niv), "but we trust in the name of the Lord our God." Sadly, David got into trouble with God when he forgot exactly where his trust should go.

It wasn't the size of David's army that had won all those battles. David defeated those enemies because God was with him, helping him. By counting his fighting men, David was showing that he trusted in his soldiers more than in God.

> "I will give you a wise and discerning heart,
> so that there will never have been anyone like
> you, nor will there ever be."
> 1 Kings 3:12 NIV

CAN I PRAY FOR GREAT WISDOM AND GET IT LIKE KING SOLOMON DID?

You can certainly pray for wisdom. God has promised to give it to you. The Bible says, "If any of you lacks wisdom, you should ask God. . .and it will be given to you" (James 1:5 TNIV). But wisdom is not the same thing as intelligence or knowledge. God won't necessarily give you a bigger IQ than He already gave you, and He won't give you a supernatural download of math knowledge so you don't have to study for a test ever again. But He will give you more wisdom.

Solomon asked God for "a discerning heart. . .to distinguish between right and wrong" (1 Kings 3:9 TNIV), so that is exactly what God gave him. Solomon needed a lot of wisdom because he had so many people to govern. You probably don't need as much wisdom as Solomon did—but ask God for what you need.

Here's the classic example of Solomon's great wisdom: He threatens to cut a baby in half to learn which of the two women claiming the child is the real mom. When one woman shouts, "Give the baby to her!" Solomon knew she was the real mother. . .and gave the child to her. Read the whole story in 1 Kings 3:16–28.

WHY WAS THE TEMPLE COMPLETELY COVERED WITH GOLD INSIDE? SHOULDN'T THAT GOLD HAVE BEEN USED TO CARE FOR THE POOR?

→

> *So Solomon overlaid the house within with pure gold.*
>
> 1 KINGS 6:21 KJV

God already had programs in place to care for widows, orphans, and the poor. In the villages and towns of Israel, the tithes of the Israelites were often distributed to feed the Levites and the poor. In Jerusalem the temple had a daily program to feed the poor. Besides, the law commanded Israelites to be generous and lend to the poor whatever they needed—and every seven years all debts were completely forgiven (Leviticus 25:35–37; Deuteronomy 14:28–29; 15:1–11).

The temple was where the Israelites met God and had their sins forgiven, so by giving valuable gold to the temple to make it beautiful, the Israelites showed that they placed great value on the place where they met God. King David was very rich, but he gave most of his gold to God, and the wealthy leaders of Israel gave generously also (1 Chronicles 29:1–9). These same rich people also gave to the poor.

Nobody knows exactly what Solomon's temple looked like, since it was destroyed almost 3,000 years ago! Other world religions still build fancy temples and cover them in gold or other shiny metals—like this Buddhist pagoda in Burma.

DID GOD ACTUALLY LIVE IN THE TEMPLE THAT SOLOMON BUILT?

→

> *"But will God really dwell on earth? The heavens, even the highest heaven, cannot contain you. How much less this temple I have built!"*
>
> 1 KINGS 8:27 TNIV

God was present in the temple Solomon built, just as He was present in the tabernacle in the wilderness. God didn't permanently live in the tabernacle, but He met with the Israelites there. The tabernacle was made of cloth, and Solomon's temple was made of stone—but neither one was big enough for God to fit in.

Solomon admitted this when he said, "Not even all of heaven is large enough to hold you, so how can this Temple that I have built be large enough?" (1 Kings 8:27 GNT). It couldn't, of course. A Christian named Stephen pointed out that God doesn't dwell in man-made temples (Acts 7:48).

Nevertheless, for many centuries, God chose the temple in Jerusalem as the place where His people were to come worship Him and offer sacrifices for sin (1 Kings 8:29; 2 Chronicles 2:6).

That changed after Jesus died for our sins. Then believers no longer needed to sacrifice or worship in Jerusalem but could worship God wherever they were (John 4:19–24).

WHY DID GOD LET SOLOMON HAVE 700 WIVES?

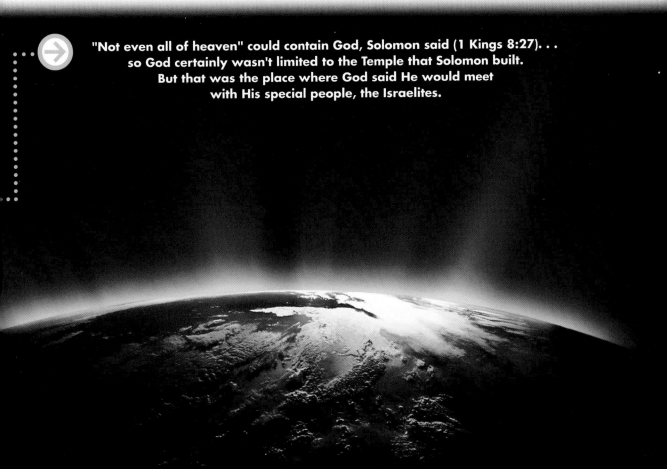

Now King Solomon loved many foreign women. . . .

1 KINGS 11:1 RSV

God didn't want Solomon to have so many wives. In fact, He had warned Israel's kings *not* to do that (Deuteronomy 17:17). But Solomon disobeyed God. He even married women who worshipped evil gods. As a result, "his wives led him astray" and "his wives turned his heart after other gods" (1 Kings 11:3–4 NIV).

It was common in those days for kings to marry the daughters of important military allies and trade partners, and Solomon probably married for business reasons in a few cases—but seriously! There were nowhere near 700 kingdoms around Israel! Solomon simply married those women because he wanted to; and because he was king, no one could stop him. As Solomon confessed, "Anything I wanted, I got. I did not deny myself any pleasure" (Ecclesiastes 2:10 GNT).

"Not even all of heaven" could contain God, Solomon said (1 Kings 8:27). . . so God certainly wasn't limited to the Temple that Solomon built. But that was the place where God said He would meet with His special people, the Israelites.

HOW COME CHRISTIANS TODAY DON'T DO GREAT MIRACLES LIKE ELIJAH AND OTHER OLD TESTAMENT PROPHETS?

Wonder-workers like Elijah have always been unique. Back in Elijah's day, there was no one else doing amazing miracles either. A few other prophets, such as Moses and Elisha, did miracles, but *most* prophets just faithfully spoke God's Word and warned people to turn to God. Even the great prophet John the Baptist did no miracles, but he did tell people about Jesus (John 10:41).

However, just because you don't hear about big miracles like the Red Sea parting doesn't mean that God isn't doing miracles in modern times. He is! Around the world, every single day, Christians are praying in Jesus' name, and God is answering their prayers and doing hundreds of thousands of "small" miracles every single day.

The LORD heard Elijah's cry, and the boy's life returned to him, and he lived. Elijah picked up the child and carried him down from the room into the house. He gave him to his mother and said, "Look, your son is alive!"

1 KINGS 17:22–23 NIV

Ever hear of somebody who was so sick she wasn't expected to live—
but then she got better? That's a kind of miracle, too!

WHY DID GOD SEND BEARS TO KILL SOME LITTLE CHILDREN WHEN ALL THEY DID WAS TEASE ELISHA?

The Bible says that as Elisha was passing the city of Bethel, "young lads came out from the city and mocked him." Then Elisha "cursed them in the name of the Lord. Then two female bears came out of the woods and tore up forty-two lads of their number" (2 Kings 2:23–24 NASB). Why would Elisha do such a thing?

The Hebrew word *yeled* translated as "young lads" actually means "youths." These were not elementary school kids playing in the school yard. This was a large gang of teenagers roaming around looking for trouble. Because there were more than 42 of them in the mob, Elisha probably felt threatened. He was alone and had no defense but God. The Lord sent two bears to punish and scare the boys. Fortunately, it seems that no one was killed. The youths most likely escaped with scratches and bites and hopefully learned a lesson.

From there Elisha went up to Bethel. As he was walking along the road, some youths came out of the town and jeered at him. "Go on up, you baldhead!" they said. "Go on up, you baldhead!" He turned around, looked at them and called down a curse on them in the name of the Lord. Then two bears came out of the woods and mauled forty-two of the youths.
2 Kings 2:23–24 NIV

HOW DID GOD MAKE AN IRON AX HEAD FLOAT?

→ He cut off a branch and tossed it at the spot. The axhead floated up.

2 KINGS 6:6 MSG

God created the world and the entire universe, so we know that He has astonishing power and imagination. God not only created the physical things that we see, but also created the invisible rules of physics that we can't see. God made the natural laws that bind electrons, neutrons, and photons together. He created matter and antimatter. He designed energy to be able to change into matter and matter to change back into energy. God created gravity and gave the earth a magnetic field.

Giant steel ships float. . .but only in very large bodies of water. It was really a miracle for a solid metal ax head to float in a small stream.

Really, when you think about it, how difficult would it have been for God to do a little anti-gravity miracle and make an iron ax head rise up from the bottom of a river?

For the Lord had caused the army of the Arameans to hear a sound of chariots and a sound of horses. . . .

2 KINGS 7:6 NASB

DOES GOD EVER TRICK PEOPLE INTO THINKING THAT SOMETHING IS TRUE WHEN IT REALLY ISN'T?

Yes, He does. One time God tricked a huge enemy army in order to protect His people. The entire army of Aram had camped around the city of Samaria in Israel. They kept anyone from going in or out of the city and waited while the Israelites slowly ran out of food and began to starve.

Magicians specialize in tricking people—making them think a rabbit suddenly appeared in their hat or that they can saw pretty ladies in half without hurting them. Even God pulled a big trick on the Arameans one time!

But in the darkness of night, God "caused the Arameans to hear the sound of chariots and horses and a great army" (2 Kings 7:6 TNIV). There was so *much* noise that the Arameans were terrified, thinking that the two greatest armies on earth—the Hittites and the Egyptians—had joined forces and were attacking them.

The Arameans fled, leaving everything behind, but there were no Hittites or Egyptian armies around. God had simply made a lot of noise.

WERE ALL THE VIOLENT THINGS KING JEHU DID GOOD OR BAD?....→

When a prophet anointed Jehu as king and told him to kill all the evil descendants of King Ahab and to uproot Baal worship from Israel, Jehu killed two evil kings and one truly wicked queen that same day. Then he ordered 70 of Ahab's male descendants beheaded. The next day, Jehu killed another 42 of Ahab's relatives. Then he called all the priests of Baal together for a "great festival" and killed them all.

> When [Jehu] came to Samaria, he killed all who remained to Ahab in Samaria, until he had destroyed him, according to the word of the LORD which He spoke to Elijah.
>
> 2 KINGS 10:17 NASB

God wanted to wipe out Baal worship in Israel, and Jehu did that (2 Kings 10:30). Jehu believed in God but still worshipped idols of the golden calf, so he was not a godly leader like King David.

But when God wanted to get rid of Baal worship, Jehu was the logical choice. He was an ambitious, get-results kind of man. Jehu had his own motivations for obeying God—namely, he wanted to be king—but God often has to use imperfect people to get the job done.

Violence is a big problem in today's world, and most of the violence that happens is *not* God's will, but the will of selfish, evil men.

Saul took a sword, and fell upon it.
1 CHRONICLES 10:4 KJV

King Saul and his armor-bearer lie dead on Mount Gilboa while other soldiers look on. The painting, by Elie Marcuse, is from the mid-1800s.

WHY DOES THE BIBLE GIVE TWO DIFFERENT STORIES OF HOW KING SAUL DIED?

King Saul died in a battle against the Philistines. First Chronicles 10:1–6 says it happened this way: When Saul was mortally wounded by Philistine archers, he decided to end his own life. So he deliberately fell on his own sword and died. The Bible says that Saul's armor-bearer *saw* him die.

However, later on, an Amalekite who claimed to be part of the Israelite army brought Saul's crown to David and told him that he had seen Saul wounded but still standing. He claimed that Saul had ordered him to kill him—so the Amalekite claimed that is what he had done (2 Samuel 1:1–16).

The first version of the story is the true one. The Amalekite was lying. In the past, Saul had tried to kill David, so the Amalekite thought David would reward him for saying that he had killed Saul. He was wrong.

Uzzah falls backward dead— after touching the ark of the covenant.

WHY WAS UZZAH KILLED FOR MERELY TRYING TO KEEP THE ARK OF THE COVENANT FROM TIPPING OVER?........➡

God is holy, and when He comes to a physical location, that spot becomes holy also. When God appeared to Moses in the burning bush, He said, "Do not come any closer," and warned that Moses was standing on "holy ground" (Exodus 3:5 NIV). God wanted the Israelites to keep a respectful distance from the ark of the covenant as well, because His Spirit was often present there.

Uzzah *knew* that he shouldn't have touched the ark. He had *heard* the story: Several years earlier, the people of Beth Shemesh had become curious, lifted the lid, and peeked inside the ark—and 70 of them had died (1 Samuel 6:19–20).

David and the priests also should have known better: They shouldn't have carried the ark on an ox cart that was liable to tip. The Levites were supposed to carry the ark on poles (Exodus 25:12–15; 1 Chronicles 15:1–2), and even *they* were forbidden to touch it or they would die (Numbers 4:15). Everyone broke the rules that day, and Uzzah paid with his life.

> David and all Israel went up to Baalah, that is, to Kiriath-jearim, which belongs to Judah, to bring up from there the ark of God, the LORD who is enthroned above the cherubim, where His name is called. They carried the ark of God on a new cart from the house of Abinadab, and Uzza and Ahio drove the cart. David and all Israel were celebrating before God with all their might, even with songs and with lyres, harps, tambourines, cymbals and with trumpets. When they came to the threshing floor of Chidon, Uzza put out his hand to hold the ark, because the oxen nearly upset it. The anger of the LORD burned against Uzza, so He struck him down because he put out his hand to the ark; and he died there before God. Then David became angry because of the LORD's outburst against Uzza; and he called that place Perez-uzza to this day. David was afraid of God that day, saying, "How can I bring the ark of God home to me?"
>
> 1 CHRONICLES 13:6–12 NASB

65

ARE DROUGHTS AND FAMINES GOD'S JUDGMENT ON SIN?

Sometimes they are, but not always. For example, in King David's day, when a drought lasted for three years, God told David that it was punishment on Israel for Saul's slaughtering of the Gibeonites, Israel's allies. When David made things right, God sent rain (2 Samuel 21). Sometimes God withheld rain when His people neglected serving Him (Haggai 1).

Other times, droughts happened simply because of changing weather patterns and because all lands in the region were going through a dry spell. In those cases, both the righteous and the unrighteous were affected. The book of Genesis describes three great droughts and doesn't mention that any was a judgment for sin (Genesis 12:10; 26:1; 41:53 –54). However, God *did* use those droughts to work out His will.

When God sends rain, He sends it on both the just and the unjust (Matthew 5:45).

"When the heavens are shut up and there is no rain because your people have sinned against you, and when they pray toward this place and confess your name and turn from their sin because you have afflicted them, then hear from heaven and forgive the sin of your servants, your people Israel. Teach them the right way to live, and send rain on the land you gave your people for an inheritance."
2 CHRONICLES 6:26–27 NIV

Droughts dry out land, kill plants. . .and starve people.

HOW COULD KING JEHORAM BE SO CRUEL AS TO KILL ALL HIS BROTHERS?

> *When Jehoram had taken over his father's kingdom and had secured his position, he killed all his brothers along with some of the government officials.*
>
> 2 CHRONICLES 21:4 MSG

Jehoshaphat was a good king, but he made a terrible mistake when he allowed his son Jehoram to marry Princess Athaliah of Israel. Athaliah was a wicked Baal worshipper, and she completely corrupted Jehoram. Jehoram turned away from the Lord and embraced the demon-god Baal. After Jehoram became king of Judah, he murdered all his brothers to keep them from challenging him for the throne.

Like many selfish, insecure rulers, he wanted no competition. Also, as the prophet Elijah pointed out, all of Jehoram's brothers were better than he was (2 Chronicles 21:13). Very likely, Jehoram worried that if he died, one of his brothers would become king and lead the people away from Baal worship and back to worshipping God.

God judged Jehoram for his evil deeds, and soon war broke out. Then the Arabs and the Philistines raided Judah and pillaged the palace. Finally, Jehoram died from a painful disease (2 Kings 8:16–22; 2 Chronicles 21).

> If you have a brother or sister, you've probably wished sometimes that you didn't. Just don't ever reach the point of sibling rivalry that Jehoram did!

HOW COULD GOOD KING JOASH TURN AGAINST GOD SO QUICKLY AND SO TOTALLY?

> *Now after the death of Jehoiada the princes of Judah came and did obeisance to the king; then the king hearkened to them. And they forsook the house of the Lord, the God of their fathers.*
>
> 2 CHRONICLES 24:17 RSV

Ever since Joash was young, he had been mentored by the high priest Jehoiada. As long as Jehoiada was alive, Joash worshipped God and did what was right. Jehoiada was a great influence for good, but many powerful officials of Judah worshipped idols. As long as Jehoiada was alive, they couldn't make their move; but as soon as he died, they influenced King Joash to worship idols—and he listened to them (2 Chronicles 24:17). Later, when Jehoiada's son spoke out against Joash's evil deeds, the palace officials plotted against him and got Joash to issue a death warrant against him.

Joash was weak and easily influenced. A later king of Judah, Zedekiah, also didn't have the backbone to resist ungodly advice (Jeremiah 38:4–6).

WHY IS THE NUMBER SEVEN SO SPECIAL?

→ *And they brought seven bullocks, and seven rams, and seven lambs, and seven he goats, for a sin offering for the kingdom, and for the sanctuary, and for Judah. And he commanded the priests the sons of Aaron to offer them on the altar of the LORD.*

2 CHRONICLES 29:21 KJV

You will often hear people say, "Seven is God's number." Actually, *all* numbers belong to God. However, the number seven does have special significance in the Bible. The Israelites sacrificed seven bulls, seven rams, seven male lambs, and seven male goats to God (2 Chronicles 29:21). The apostle John describes seven stars, seven lampstands, seven spirits of God, seven seals, seven trumpets, and seven plagues (Revelation 1:12, 16; 4:5; 5:1; 8:6; 15:1). Even Jesus is described as a Lamb with seven horns and seven eyes (Revelation 5:6).

The number seven symbolizes completeness and perfection. It is based on the fact that seven days make one complete week, and that God rested on the seventh day "and made it holy" (Genesis 2:2–3).

IF WE KEEP ON SINNING, DOES THERE COME A POINT AT WHICH THERE IS NO MORE HOPE OF REPENTANCE AND MERCY?

→ *The wrath of the LORD was aroused against his people and there was no remedy.*

2 CHRONICLES 36:16 TNIV

In Jeremiah's day, the people of Judah were disobedient to the Lord. But because God had great compassion, He kept sending prophets to warn them. Still, they refused to change. "They kept mocking the messengers of God, despising his words, and scoffing at his prophets, till the wrath of the LORD rose against his people, till there was no remedy" (2 Chronicles 36:16 RSV).

God is love, and He gave His people many, many chances to change their ways. But when they stubbornly refused to listen, they had to suffer the consequences. Of course, *after* God punished His people and they finally woke up and repented, He once again had mercy on them and restored them.

Jeremiah was called the "weeping prophet" for the tears he cried over his people. Their stubbornness led to an invasion by a foreign country, and many of the Jewish people were carried off from their country.

WHY DID PERSIA'S KING CYRUS ALLOW THE JEWS TO RETURN TO THEIR HOMELAND?

The Babylonians uprooted people from their homelands if the people rebelled against them, and resettled them in distant lands to discourage them from rebelling again. The Persians were more tolerant, however. They believed that if they governed people fairly, the people wouldn't rebel. They even allowed captive peoples like the Jews to go back to their homelands.

This fulfilled a prophecy that God had given Isaiah. Hundreds of years before the Persian Empire existed, God prophesied that He would make a man named Cyrus set the Jews free to go rebuild Jerusalem (Isaiah 45:1–4, 13). When Cyrus came along, that is exactly what he did (Ezra 1:1–3).

In the first year of Cyrus king of Persia, in order to fulfill the word of the LORD spoken by Jeremiah, the LORD moved the heart of Cyrus king of Persia. . . .

EZRA 1:1 TNIV

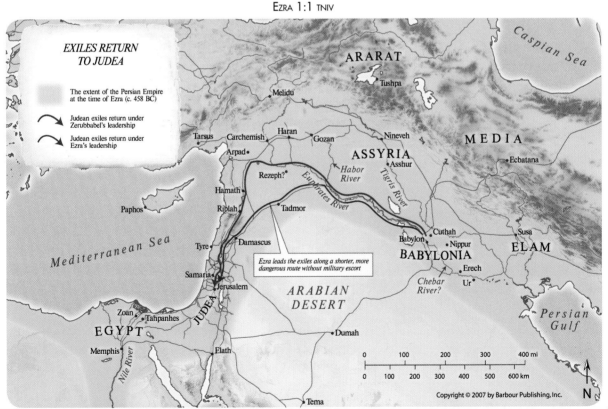

EXILES RETURN TO JUDEA

The extent of the Persian Empire at the time of Ezra (c. 458 BC)

Judean exiles return under Zerubbabel's leadership

Judean exiles return under Ezra's leadership

Ezra leads the exiles along a shorter, more dangerous route without military escort

Copyright © 2007 by Barbour Publishing, Inc.

WHY WAS iT SO iMPORTANT FOR THE JEWS TO REBUiLD THE TEMPLE?.........➡

The Babylonians attacked Israel, tore down the temple of God, and took the Jews far away to Babylon. For 70 years, the Jews had no temple, so they began meeting together every Sabbath to pray, worship God, and read the Scriptures. That's how synagogues (meeting houses) began. When the Jews returned to Israel, they continued meeting in synagogues.

> Let him go up to Jerusalem, which is in Judah, and build the house of the LORD God of Israel, (he is the God,) which is in Jerusalem.
>
> EZRA 1:3 KJV

This was a good thing, but something was missing. The Messiah, Jesus, hadn't yet come to die for their sins—so the Jews still needed animal sacrifices to cover their sins and restore a relationship with God. The only place they were allowed to sacrifice was at the altar in the temple (Deuteronomy 12:5–14), so they had to rebuild the altar and the temple as soon as possible (Ezra 3:1–10).

WHY WAS EZRA SO ANGRY ABOUT JEWS MARRYiNG NON-JEWS?...............................➡

More than 3,000 years ago, God made a rule for His people—the Jews—that they only marry other Jews. Here's what a Jewish wedding looked like a hundred years ago.

God had commanded the Israelites not to marry the people of Canaan (Deuteronomy 7:3–4). He explained why: "You shall not enter into marriage

> "The people of Israel and the priests and the Levites have not separated themselves from the peoples of the lands. . . . For they have taken some of their daughters as wives for themselves and their sons."
>
> EZRA 9:1–2 NKJV

with them. . .for surely they will turn away your heart after their gods" (1 Kings 11:2 RSV). King Solomon, the wisest man on earth, thought that *he* could marry pagan wives and get away with it—but next thing you know, he was worshipping their wicked gods to please them (1 Kings 11:3–9; Nehemiah 13:26).

Later on, most Jews ended up worshipping pagan gods. This made God so angry that He allowed the Babylonians to attack Israel and take the people from their land for 70 years. Now that God had again shown mercy to the Jews and allowed them to return to their homeland, Ezra didn't want to see them fall back into idol worship.

WHY WAS IT SO IMPORTANT TO BUILD A WALL AROUND JERUSALEM?

The Jews were back in their own land and living in Jerusalem, but they were in great trouble because the walls of the city were broken down (Nehemiah 1:3). There were lots of Samaritans and Ammonites and Arabs and Philistines living around them who were harassing them. If their enemies attacked, the Jews needed to be able to flee inside a city with high stone walls around it to be safe. As long as Jerusalem's walls were broken down, they had no refuge.

Also, they needed to protect God's temple from enemies who despised God. That's why when Nehemiah became governor, he made it his first priority to rebuild the city's walls.

Daniel had prophesied that the wall would "be built again. . .in troublesome times" (Daniel 9:25 NKJV), and it was.

Then Eliashib the high priest rose up with his brethren the priests and they built the Sheep Gate. They consecrated it and set its doors; they consecrated it as far as the Tower of the Hundred, as far as the Tower of Hananel. And next to him the men of Jericho built. And next to them Zaccur the son of Imri built. And the sons of Hassenaah built the Fish Gate; they laid its beams and set its doors, its bolts, and its bars. And next to them Meremoth the son of Uriah, son of Hakkoz repaired. And next to them Meshullam the son of Berechiah, son of Meshezabel repaired. And next to them Zadok the son of Baana repaired. And next to them the Tekoites repaired. . . .
NEHEMIAH 3:1–5 RSV

If you visit the Holy Lands today, you'll see walls like this around the "old city" of Jerusalem.

WHY DID SOME PARENTS IN OLD TESTAMENT TIMES SELL THEIR CHILDREN AS SLAVES?......

Some parents sold their children as slaves because they were desperately poor and had no other way to get money for food or to pay their debts (2 Kings 4:1). Slavery is a terrible thing, but at least Jewish masters weren't allowed to make Jewish servants work too hard or do humiliating work. Also, the law said that Jewish servants had to be set free after seven years (Exodus 21:2; Leviticus 25:39–43).

Some parents complained to Nehemiah that they had been forced to sell their sons and daughters as slaves because rich Jews had taken over their farms—making them even poorer. And instead of giving them interest-free loans, the rich Jews had been charging them interest, forcing them even deeper into debt.

Nehemiah was furious and told the people that they hadn't paid to free Jewish slaves from the heathen just to see their children sold as slaves to fellow Jews. He demanded that the rich give the poor back their lands and stop charging interest (Nehemiah 5:1–12).

Now the men and their wives raised a great outcry against their Jewish brothers. Some were saying, "We and our sons and daughters are numerous; in order for us to eat and stay alive, we must get grain." Others were saying, "We are mortgaging our fields, our vineyards and our homes to get grain during the famine." Still others were saying, "We have had to borrow money to pay the king's tax on our fields and vineyards. Although we are of the same flesh and blood as our countrymen and though our sons are as good as theirs, yet we have to subject our sons and daughters to slavery. Some of our daughters have already been enslaved, but we are powerless, because our fields and our vineyards belong to others."

NEHEMIAH 5:1–5 NIV

Two girls protest the "slavery" of American children in 1909. . .the conditions that forced some families to send young kids into the workplace. Eventually, laws were made to prohibit "child labor." Jewish families of Old Testament times would have approved!

WHY IS GOD NEVER MENTIONED IN THE BOOK OF ESTHER?

The word *God* or *Lord* appears in every book of the Bible except for the book of Esther. Some people worry that this means the book of Esther wasn't inspired by God. Or they think that Esther isn't a very spiritual book. Yet when you read it, you see that it is a very inspired book. When Esther and all the Jews were facing a life-and-death situation, they fasted for three days (Esther 4:15–16). They weren't fasting to lose weight; they were fasting and praying desperately for God to help them. In Jewish culture, fasting always meant "a fast before the LORD" (Jeremiah 36:9 NKJV). The good news is that God answered their prayers and saved the Jews from their enemies.

Mordecai talks with Esther, in a 1685 painting by Aert de Gelder.

WHY DID GOD ALLOW JOB TO SUFFER SO MUCH?

Job was a righteous man who tried his best to please God. The Lord in turn blessed Job with wealth and health, and put a protective barrier around him and everything he owned. The devil wanted to bring Job trouble and sickness but couldn't get through, so he argued that Job only feared God because God had blessed him. The devil insisted that if God took away Job's wealth and health, Job would curse Him (Job 1:1–12; 2:1–7).

God hated to see Job suffer, but to prove Satan wrong, He allowed Job to be tested. Job passed the tests and came out even stronger and more blessed than ever (Job 42:12–16).

God also allowed Satan to test the apostle Peter. Even though Peter failed the test and denied Jesus, in the end he, too, came out stronger and more pure-hearted and became the leader of the disciples (Luke 22:31–34; Acts 2:14).

Job, diseased and depressed, gets some advice from his wife: "Curse God and die!" (Job 2:9 NIV). It was bad advice, to be sure—but don't forget that she was driven insane with grief. Not only was her husband terribly sick; she'd also lost her 10 kids and all the family wealth.

> "Naked I came from my mother's womb, and naked I will depart. The LORD gave and the LORD has taken away; may the name of the LORD be praised. In all this, Job did not sin by charging God with wrongdoing.
>
> JOB 1:21–22 NIV

WERE JOB'S THREE FRIENDS RIGHT WHEN THEY SAID GOD WAS JUDGING JOB FOR HIS SINS?

No. They were wrong. Job was a righteous man who loved God. The Lord allowed Job to suffer because He knew that it would make Job a more deeply spiritual man. However, God *does* punish people for their sins. When people ignore God, He allows trouble to come into their lives. When they obey God, He blesses them. When they disobey, He judges them (Deuteronomy 28).

Job's friends knew these basic spiritual laws, so they assumed that God must be punishing Job. Even though they couldn't think of anything Job had done wrong, they insisted that there must be *some* sin! They then began falsely accusing Job of all kinds of terrible things.

Finally, a fourth friend became angry with the other three because they had condemned Job even though they couldn't prove he'd done anything wrong (Job 32:3).

The boastful may not stand before thy eyes; thou hatest all evildoers. Thou destroyest those who speak lies; the LORD abhors bloodthirsty and deceitful men.
PSALM 5:5–6 RSV

iF GOD iS LOVE, WHY DO THE PSALMS SAY THAT GOD HATES EVILDOERS?

The Bible tells us that "God is love" (1 John 4:8) and that God loved us so much that He sent Jesus to die for us (John 3:16). All people are sinners, yet God loves people even while they're sinning (Romans 3:23; 5:8). Yet the Bible also clearly states, "Thou hatest all evildoers. . . . The LORD abhors bloodthirsty and deceitful men" (Psalm 5:5–6 RSV).

How can God love sinners but hate evildoers? There's a difference. Some people sin from time to time, some people sin often, but *some* people are thoroughly wicked: They hate God, delight to do evil, and work hard at it all day long. They are sadistic, bloodthirsty people who enjoy murdering and causing pain. These are the evildoers God hates.

And yet, if they repent and turn from their evil ways, God can save even the wickedest people—like the apostle Paul (Acts 26:9–11; 1 Timothy 1:15).

A lightning bolt is a common image used for God's anger. . . just like King David wrote in 2 Samuel 22:15 (NIV)—
"He shot arrows and scattered the enemies, bolts of lightning and routed them."

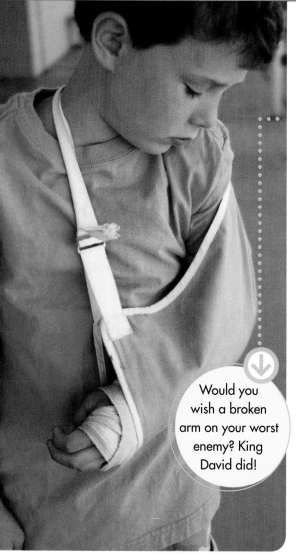

Would you wish a broken arm on your worst enemy? King David did!

WHY DID DAVID PRAY MEAN PRAYERS, SUCH AS, "GOD, BREAK THE ARMS OF THE WICKED"? ..... ⬇

David prayed such a strong prayer for a very good reason. He wasn't praying against people

> Break thou the arm of the wicked and evildoer; seek out his wickedness till thou find none.
>
> PSALM 10:15 RSV

who had simply knocked his books over or had said something mean to offend him. He was praying against hardened criminals. If you read the verses before this one, you will see that these men hunted down the weak, praised the greedy, cursed the Lord, proudly thought they were invincible, constantly told lies, threatened others, set ambushes to murder the innocent, and dragged off their helpless victims and crushed them. And while their victims were crying out to God, the wicked laughed, "God will never notice!" (Psalm 10:1–13 TNIV).

Of course David prayed, "Break the arms of the wicked and the evildoers!" If their arms were broken, they wouldn't be able to keep doing so much evil.

⁞ IF YOU TRULY LOVE GOD, WILL HE KEEP ALL TROUBLE OUT OF YOUR LIFE? ....

> → The righteous cry out, and the LORD hears them; he delivers them from all their troubles.
>
> PSALM 34:17 NIV

David said, "The righteous call to the Lord, and he listens; he rescues them from all their troubles" (Psalm 34:17 GNT). Some Christians think—or they wish!—that this means that if they love God and live righteously, He will keep all trouble out of their lives. They then feel as if God has let them down when they go through periods of trouble.

But this verse isn't saying our lives will always be easy. In fact, only two verses later, the Bible says, "Good people suffer *many* troubles, but the Lord saves them from them all" (Psalm 34:19 GNT, emphasis added). As a Christian, you can expect to face many troubles (Acts 14:22). It may

take time, and you may have to endure some troubles for a while, but God will "save" you from all of them—when He takes you to heaven, where there is no trouble at all!

The apostle Paul loved God—but he never escaped the problems of life: "Five times I received from the Jews the forty lashes minus one. Three times I was beaten with rods, once I was stoned, three times I was shipwrecked, I spent a night and a day in the open sea, I have been constantly on the move. I have been in danger from rivers, in danger from bandits, in danger from my own countrymen, in danger from Gentiles; in danger in the city, in danger in the country, in danger at sea; and in danger from false brothers" (2 CORINTHIANS 11:24–26 NIV).

WILL GOD ALWAYS SUPPLY EVERYTHING YOU WANT?....

David said, "Take delight in the LORD, and he will give you the desires of your heart" (Psalm 37:4 RSV). He

> Delight yourself in the LORD and he will give you the desires of your heart.
> PSALM 37:4 NIV

also said, "Those who seek the LORD lack no good thing" (Psalm 34:10 RSV).

These verses seem to promise that if you love God and seek Him, He will give you whatever "good thing" you pray for—so if you desire a new PSP or iPod, God will see to it that you get it, right? Not necessarily. When you truly delight in God and His ways, your desires *change* from wanting fun things just for

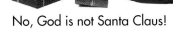

No, God is not Santa Claus!

your own personal pleasure to wanting what God knows is best for you.

Besides, as Paul said, "My God will supply every need of yours" (Philippians 4:19 RSV). God will supply what you *need*, but He wants you to be content with what He gives you, whether it's exactly what you wanted or not, whether it's little or much (Philippians 4:11–12; 1 Timothy 6:6–9).

WOULD GOD REALLY "CAST AWAY" SOMEONE WHO BELIEVES IN HIM?

> ⮕ *Because of your great wrath, for you have taken me up and thrown me aside.*
> PSALM 102:10 TNIV

Ever feel all alone? Lots of people in the Bible felt that way, too—but God has promised He'll always be with us.

In Psalm 102, a believer cries out to God, "You have lifted me up and cast me away" (verse 10 NKJV). Does this mean that God casts people away forever, not letting them enter heaven? No. The title of the psalm reads, "A prayer of the afflicted." When you read the entire psalm, it's clear that "afflicted" refers to people who are sick or being oppressed by their enemies; people who *feel* as if God is judging them, picking them up, and throwing them away.

Job felt the same way when he was sick. He said that God had picked him up and tossed him into the mud (Job 30:19). Had God actually done such a thing? No, but when God allowed Job to suffer, Job *felt* as if God had discarded him. In actuality, God has promised never to leave us nor forsake us (Hebrews 13:5).

> *Praise ye the LORD. Blessed is the man that feareth the LORD, that delighteth greatly in his commandments.*
> PSALM 112:1 KJV ⬅

WHY SHOULD WE FEAR GOD? ISN'T HE OUR LOVING FATHER?

David says, "Blessed is the man who fears the LORD" (Psalm 112:1 NIV). Many people wonder why it's a *good* thing to fear God. After all, God is compassionate and loves us; He's our heavenly Father and only wants good for us, so why should we fear Him? Isn't fear a negative thing?

No, not always. In this case "fear" means having a very healthy respect for God.

God is a loving God, but He is all-powerful and He hates sin, so we are very wise if we fear to disobey Him. You wouldn't throw stones at a tiger and then crawl into its cage, right? Having a healthy respect for the tiger is a wise thing. Well, God is far more powerful, and He tells us, "The fear of the LORD is the *beginning* of wisdom" (Proverbs 9:10 NIV, emphasis added). Yes, God loves you and sent Jesus to die for your sins, but it's not wise to deliberately anger Him.

WHY DO THE PSALMS TELL US OVER AND OVER TO PRAISE GOD? DOES GOD ENJOY HEARING US CONSTANTLY TELL HIM HOW GREAT HE IS?

God is so immensely powerful that He created the entire universe—every star, every planet, and every living thing. When we understand how mind-bogglingly awesome God is, and that He's the one who created us, it dawns on us that we should worship Him. And it's natural to *say* what we're thinking and praise Him.

Praising God is not like praising other people to make them feel good about themselves. God doesn't have an ego problem. We praise God because all the wonderful things we're saying about Him are *true!*

The most important commandment is this: "Love the Lord your God with all your heart and with all your soul and with all your mind" (Matthew 22:37 TNIV). If you love God *that* much, you're already worshipping Him. And if you love God with everything in you and appreciate all that He's done for you, how can you *help* but praise Him (2 Corinthians 4:13)?

Praise ye the LORD. Praise God in his sanctuary: praise him in the firmament of his power. Praise him for his mighty acts: praise him according to his excellent greatness. Praise him with the sound of the trumpet: praise him with the psaltery and harp. Praise him with the timbrel and dance: praise him with stringed instruments and organs. Praise him upon the loud cymbals: praise him upon the high sounding cymbals. Let every thing that hath breath praise the LORD. Praise ye the LORD.

PSALM 150 KJV

WHAT IS WISDOM? ......→

Solomon writes, "Getting wisdom is the most important thing you can do" (Proverbs 4:7 GNT). Why is getting wisdom so important? And what exactly is wisdom? Well, wisdom is more than just getting knowledge or memorizing facts. If that were all it was, then studying history or science would be the most important thing you could do. Those things are important, but getting wisdom is the most important.

> The beginning of wisdom is this: Get wisdom. Though it cost all you have, get understanding.
>
> PROVERBS 4:7 TNIV

When Solomon prayed for wisdom, he asked God for "a discerning heart. . .to distinguish between right and wrong" (1 Kings 3:9 TNIV). To "discern" means to see into the heart of a matter. Real wisdom means to speak not only with knowledge but also with love. Anyone can memorize facts and figures, but a wise person understands how to use knowledge to solve problems and help others.

SHOULD MODERN WOMEN AND GIRLS BEHAVE LIKE WOMEN OF ANCIENT TIMES? ....⊙

Some Christians believe that the Bible teaches that a husband should have the final say in any discussion—that wives should always submit to their husbands (Colossians 3:18). They believe that, even today, women are not supposed to teach men, nor even to speak out loud in church (1 Timothy 2:12; 1 Corinthians 14:34). Some even insist that women must cover their heads when they pray (1 Corinthians 11:5–6).

> Charm is deceitful and beauty is passing, but a woman who fears the LORD, she shall be praised.
>
> PROVERBS 31:30 NKJV

Other Christians agree that that's the way it (mostly) was in olden days, but that even in the Old Testament, women had freedom and led God's people (Proverbs 31; Judges 4:1–8). They especially believe that ever since Jesus died, there is no difference in the roles of males and females (Galatians 3:28), that husbands and wives are partners, "heirs together" of eternal life (1 Peter 3:7).

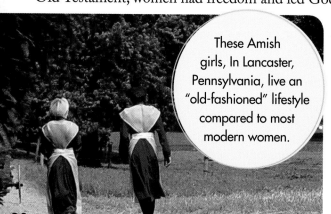

These Amish girls, In Lancaster, Pennsylvania, live an "old-fashioned" lifestyle compared to most modern women.

Different churches have different views, so it would be good to ask what your parents and pastors believe. They have probably thought about it a great deal.

"Meaningless! Meaningless!" says the Teacher.
"Utterly meaningless! Everything is meaningless."
ECCLESIASTES 1:2 NIV

WHY IS ECCLESIASTES SUCH A SAD, DISCOURAGING BOOK?

Solomon writes, "Everything is meaningless. . . . I have seen all the things that are done under the sun; all of them are meaningless, a chasing after the wind" (Ecclesiastes 1:2, 14 TNIV). He asks what people gain from a lifetime of work, because one day they'll die and leave it behind. It's like chasing the wind: If you try to grab the air, in the end you have nothing. If this world is all there is, what's the point in living?

This life is *not* all there is. Solomon says at the end of Ecclesiastes that we should love and obey God, because one day God will judge us for every deed—good and evil (12:13–14).

So do good and be satisfied with what you have, "for we brought nothing into this world, and it is certain we can carry nothing out" (1 Timothy 6:7 NKJV). That's why Jesus said to store up spiritual riches in heaven rather than hoarding material things on earth (Matthew 6:19–21).

**For Christians, the cemetery isn't the end—
it's just the beginning of real life!**

IF KNOWLEDGE BRINGS GRIEF AND SORROW, WHY GO TO SCHOOL?......

Solomon writes, "With much wisdom comes much sorrow; the more knowledge, the more grief" (Ecclesiastes 1:18 NIV). Some people ask, "If that's the case, why go to school? Why learn anything if knowledge just makes you sad?" But does that mean it's best to be ignorant?

> For with much wisdom comes much sorrow; the more knowledge, the more grief.
>
> ECCLESIASTES 1:18 NIV

No, that's not what Solomon meant. Knowledge is good. You need to get a good education, and Solomon himself says that wisdom is the most important thing you can have (Proverbs 4:7).

But as you grow up, you learn, as Solomon did, that there is a lot of injustice in the world. Life is often not fair (Ecclesiastes 3:16–17; 4:1–3). Good people suffer poverty and are oppressed by corrupt governments. Innocent people die in earthquakes. Murders and robberies happen every day. Knowing that 12 x 10 = 120 won't make you sad; but watch enough news on TV, and it's bound to make you "wiser but sadder."

WHY DOES SOLOMON SAY THAT THERE ARE TIMES TO KILL, TO TEAR DOWN, AND TO HATE?........

Solomon said there is a time for everything, a time for every different kind of activity and emotional reaction. There is "a time to be born and a time to die. . .a time to weep and a time to laugh. . .a time to keep silence and

> For everything there is a season. . . .
>
> ECCLESIASTES 3:1 RSV

a time to speak" (Ecclesiastes 3:2, 4, 7 NIV). These things are true, right? You shouldn't stay silent when it's time to speak up, but you shouldn't butt in and speak when something is none of your business.

Just so, there is also a time to build and a time to tear down old, rotten buildings that are no longer safe to live in. There is a time for our nation to be at peace with other nations, and there are times when our armed forces must go to war and fight. There is a time to love someone's good deeds and a time to hate evil deeds and injustice. We need the wisdom to know how to react in different circumstances.

Every year is filled with seasons—and so is every life. Ecclesiastes teaches that every human emotion and activity has its own "season."

WHY DID SOLOMON WRITE A BOOK ALL ABOUT ROMANCE?

Solomon wrote the words to a very long song called the Song of Songs. Today we have just the words without the music. Solomon wrote this beautiful, imaginative love song for his wife, and—no surprise—men and women who are in love and married often get a lot out of reading it. They're glad to learn that God is okay with them feeling romantic and sighing and kissing. They're happy to read that physical love between a husband and wife is pure in God's eyes. Just as there is a time for everything, when you are older, there will be a time for the Song of Songs.

Ew, gross! Why do grown-ups have to be so mushy? You'll figure it out in a few years. . . .

The Song—best of all songs—Solomon's song! The Woman: Kiss me—full on the mouth! Yes! For your love is better than wine, headier than your aromatic oils. The syllables of your name murmur like a meadow brook. No wonder everyone loves to say your name!
SONG OF SONGS 1:1–3 MSG

This building, called the Hagia Maria Sion Abbey, stands atop Mount Zion today.

WHAT IS THE MOUNTAIN OF THE LORD'S HOUSE?

Mount Zion is a very small mountain—really just a hill—inside the city of Jerusalem, on which Solomon's temple was built. Because the temple was also called "the Lord's house," "the mountain of the Lord's house" referred to Mount Zion, where the temple stood.

Isaiah prophesied, "The mountain where the Temple stands will be the highest one of all, towering above all the hills" (Isaiah 2:2 GNT). Isaiah didn't mean that the temple mountain would erupt like a volcano and grow bigger. He was using symbolic language to describe God reigning over all the earth. Physically, Mount Zion is not big, but spiritually, it is the highest mountain on earth, because God will reign there.

Many peoples will come and say, "Come, let us go up to the mountain of the LORD, to the house of the God of Jacob. He will teach us his ways, so that we may walk in his paths." The law will go out from Zion, the word of the LORD from Jerusalem.
ISAIAH 2:3 NIV

Want to know your future? Don't go to a fortune-teller!

WHAT DOES THE BIBLE SAY ABOUT GOING TO MEDIUMS?

And when they say to you, "Seek those who are mediums and wizards, who whisper and mutter," should not a people seek their God? Should they seek the dead on behalf of the living?

ISAIAH 8:19 NKJV

Today many people think that going to a medium is harmless and even helpful, but God condemns this. He says, "Do not turn to mediums or seek out spiritists, for you will be defiled by them" (Leviticus 19:31 NIV). *Defiled* means to become filthy. God warns that He will turn against those who consult mediums (Leviticus 20:6).

The ancient Egyptians constantly sought advice from spirits. To prove that He was God, the Lord said He would foil the Egyptians' plans and punish them (Isaiah 19:3–4). King Saul lost the kingdom, and his life, for consulting a medium at Endor (1 Samuel 28:5–19).

God said, "When someone tells you to consult mediums and spiritists, who whisper and mutter, should not a people inquire of their God?" (Isaiah 8:19 TNIV). The answer, of course, is a definite "Yes!" Pray to God. Stay far away from mediums.

"By his wounds we are healed" (ISAIAH 53:5 NIV).

WHY DO PEOPLE SAY THAT ISAIAH 53 IS A PROPHECY ABOUT JESUS?

Isaiah was a prophet, and he spoke accurately about things that would happen in the future. Some things he prophesied came to pass during his lifetime; other prophecies were fulfilled after he died.

Isaiah's most amazing prophecy is recorded in Isaiah 53. It was written some 700 years before Jesus lived, yet it describes Jesus' trial, death, and burial in astonishing detail. It even describes why He died— to take away our sins.

In the New Testament, the Gospels describe

how Jesus fulfilled Isaiah's prophecy. Compare Isaiah 53:1 with John 12:38, and Isaiah 53:7 with Matthew 27:12–14. An early Christian named Philip declared that Isaiah 53:7–8 refers to Jesus (Acts 8:32–33)—and it does! If you've never read Isaiah 53, read it today.

> *Surely he hath borne our griefs, and carried our sorrows: yet we did esteem him stricken, smitten of God, and afflicted. But he was wounded for our transgressions, he was bruised for our iniquities: the chastisement of our peace was upon him; and with his stripes we are healed.*
>
> ISAIAH 53:4–5 KJV

IF PEOPLE WON'T STOP SINNING, DOES GOD REFUSE TO HEAR THEIR PRAYERS?

> *Look! Listen! God's arm is not amputated—he can still save. God's ears are not stopped up—he can still hear. There's nothing wrong with God; the wrong is in you. Your wrongheaded lives caused the split between you and God. Your sins got between you so that he doesn't hear.*
>
> ISAIAH 59:1–2 MSG

Yes, if by "hear" you mean hear *and answer*. God sees everything people do and hears everything they say. But when people rebel against God and stubbornly refuse to obey Him, if they keep on sinning, at some point God stops answering their prayers. The Bible says, "Your iniquities have separated you from your God; and your sins have hidden His face from you, so that He will not hear" (Isaiah 59:2 NKJV). Once they repent, however, God forgives them and answers their prayers again.

Don't be quick to judge people, though. Just because God isn't answering someone's prayer (yet) doesn't mean that person is sinning. Remember, that's what Job's friends falsely accused him of. Sometimes it simply takes *time* for prayer to be answered. Perhaps God is testing that person's faith. Or perhaps what they're asking for isn't God's will for them, but He still loves them very much.

However, if people know that they're displeasing God, then, yes, they need to stop displeasing Him.

DO NOT DISTURB

WHY DID GOD LET THE PAGAN BABYLONIANS CONQUER HIS OWN PEOPLE, THE JEWS?

God had promised in Moses' day—before the Israelites even entered the Promised Land—that as long as His people loved Him and obeyed Him, He would bless them and protect them. At the same time, however, God warned the Israelites that if they disobeyed Him and began to worship other gods, He would judge them. He would allow enemies to invade and conquer them and even take them from their land (Deuteronomy 28).

> I am calling all the tribes of the kingdoms of the north, says the LORD; and they shall come and every one shall set his throne at the entrance of the gates of Jerusalem.
>
> JEREMIAH 1:15 RSV

The Jews knew God's warning but willfully chose to disobey Him and worship other gods. So the Lord brought the Babylonians to conquer them (Jeremiah 1:14–16). This punishment taught the Jews a very good lesson. After they returned to their land 70 years later, they were determined to worship only God.

WHY DIDN'T THE JEWS LISTEN TO THE PROPHET JEREMIAH?

> I am ridiculed all day long; everyone mocks me.
>
> JEREMIAH 20:7 NIV

Many Jews worshipped Baal and other gods, so they didn't want to listen to a prophet of God telling them that they should destroy their "evil idols" and worship only the Lord. Many who worshipped Ishtar—the Queen of Heaven—believed that this goddess was blessing them and argued that if they stopped worshipping her, they'd lose their blessings (Jeremiah 44:15–18). They'd actually lost out by not worshipping God!

Also, many people in Judah were still going through the motions of worshipping God, so they thought that everything was okay. But God said, "Judah has not turned to Me with her whole heart, but in pretense" (Jeremiah 3:10 NKJV). Jeremiah added, "They always speak well of you, yet they do not really care about you" (Jeremiah 12:2 GNT).

Worse yet, some false prophets proclaimed that God would still bless them and convinced the disobedient Jews that they didn't need to listen to Jeremiah or repent (Jeremiah 28).

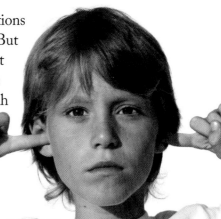

> *Arise, cry out in the night, as the watches of the night begin; pour out your heart like water in the presence of the Lord. Lift up your hands to him for the lives of your children, who faint from hunger at the head of every street.*
> **LAMENTATIONS 2:19** NIV

IF GOD IS ALL-POWERFUL, WHY DOES HE ALLOW CHILDREN TO SUFFER?

Around the world, people are suffering and going hungry. In some nations, evil rulers fight wars that bring death and starvation to their people. Others foolishly waste money and cause poverty. If God is all-powerful, why doesn't He stop this? Why does He allow innocent people to suffer—even children? Well, God *will* set things right, when Jesus returns and rules righteously.

But what about disasters like droughts and earthquakes and the AIDS epidemic? Why does God allow such things? They happen because we live in an imperfect world. Rather than blame God for them, we need to pray. Jeremiah writes, "Pour out your heart like water before the presence of the Lord. . .for the lives of your children, who faint for hunger" (Lamentations 2:19 RSV).

God wants us to pray for those who suffer—*and* He wants us to help them. That's why Christians should work to overcome poverty, help discover cures for diseases, and find peaceful ways to settle conflicts. And that's why we should donate money, if we can, to help victims of earthquakes, famines, and other disasters (see James 2:15–16; 1 John 3:17–18). God will reward us for helping others (Matthew 25:31–40).

Many children around the world go to bed hungry, sick, and alone. Have you thanked God for all He's

> I am the man who has seen affliction by the rod of His wrath. He has led me and made me walk in darkness and not in light. Surely He has turned His hand against me time and time again throughout the day. He has aged my flesh and my skin, and broken my bones. He has besieged me and surrounded me with bitterness and woe.
>
> LAMENTATIONS 3:1–5 NKJV

IS IT OKAY TO COMPLAIN TO GOD WHEN WE PRAY?

The apostle Paul said, "Do everything without complaining," and "Ask God for what you need, always asking him with a thankful heart" (Philippians 2:14; 4:6 GNT). The Lord doesn't enjoy hearing selfish prayers, such as, "God, if you don't give me a new game system, I won't love you anymore."

However, God understands that when some people go through very difficult experiences, they think that He doesn't love them anymore. He understands that when they're in pain, they cry out, asking why He allows them to suffer. Men in the Bible, such as Job and Ethan the Ezrahite, prayed gloomy prayers when they were suffering (Job 3; 9; Psalm 89:38–51), yet they still praised God (Job 1:21; Psalm 89:52).

Jeremiah complained that God had shut out his prayer and attacked him—yet he concluded that God was good and compassionate (Lamentations 3:1–36).

God doesn't like to hear complaints, but He also knows if you're only pretending to be trusting and cheerful. He'd rather you prayed an *honest* prayer, even when you're feeling miserable.

Fair

Not so Great

There were figures resembling four living beings. . . .
EZEKIEL 1:5 NASB

WHAT ARE CHERUBIM?

When Ezekiel had a vision of God on His throne, he saw four cherubim around Him. Each of the cherubim had a body like a man, but with four heads: one head like a man, another like a lion, another like an ox, and another like an eagle. The cherubim had four wings, and their entire bodies were covered with eyes. They had feet like oxen and hands like men, looked like burning coals of fire, and moved like flashes of lightning (Ezekiel 1:4–14).

When John saw them, the cherubim stood around God's throne like royal, ceremonial guards—sort of like the lions some kings kept chained near their thrones. The cherubim also never stop praising God (Revelation 4:6–9).

Many people think that cherubim are a kind of angel, but the Bible actually refers to them as "beasts" or "creatures" or "living beings." It would be best to think of the cherubim as awesome spiritual beings. (See also Ezekiel 10:1–17.)

Many people think of a "cherub" as a cute little angel with wings— but that's not how the Bible describes them!

In a way, Ezekiel was an actor—playing a role God had given him for the benefit of all who would watch him. Sadly, very few cared about his message.

WHY DID THE PROPHET EZEKIEL DO SO MANY STRANGE THINGS?

When you read the book of Ezekiel, you see how many unusual things God told Ezekiel to do. First, Ezekiel made a tiny, detailed model of the Babylonian army camped around Jerusalem. Then he lay on his left side for 390 days (that's more than a year!) staring at it. Next, he made a fire from cow dung and cooked his food over it. He also cut off his beard and shaved his head bald. Then Ezekiel dug a hole through the wall of his house and carried all his stuff out through the hole. Finally, when Ezekiel's beloved wife died, God told him not to publicly mourn her—so Ezekiel didn't (Ezekiel 4; 5; 12; 24:15–27).

God had Ezekiel do these startling "skits" to get the Jews' attention. The prophet Jeremiah had warned them for many years what would happen to them if they continued to disobey God, but the Jews hadn't listened. So God gave Ezekiel not only messages to speak but messages to act out. Ezekiel told the disobedient Jews that what he was doing was a symbol of what God would do to them (Ezekiel 12:11).

Dig thou through the wall in their sight, and carry out thereby. In their sight shalt thou bear it upon thy shoulders, and carry it forth in the twilight: thou shalt cover thy face, that thou see not the ground: for I have set thee for a sign unto the house of Israel. And I did so as I was commanded: I brought forth my stuff by day, as stuff for captivity, and in the even I digged through the wall with mine hand; I brought it forth in the twilight, and I bare it upon my shoulder in their sight. And in the morning came the word of the LORD unto me, saying, Son of man, hath not the house of Israel, the rebellious house, said unto thee, What doest thou? Say thou unto them, Thus saith the Lord GOD; This burden concerneth the prince in Jerusalem, and all the house of Israel that are among them. Say, I am your sign: like as I have done, so shall it be done unto them: they shall remove and go into captivity. And the prince that is among them shall bear upon his shoulder in the twilight, and shall go forth: they shall dig through the wall to carry out thereby: he shall cover his face, that he see not the ground with his eyes.

EZEKIEL 12:5–12 KJV

WHAT DOES EZEKIEL'S WEIRD VISION ABOUT DRY BONES MEAN?.... →

This was one of the weirdest visions Ezekiel ever had, yet it is filled with beautiful meaning. Through the Holy Spirit, God took Ezekiel to a valley full of scattered, dry bones. Then, when Ezekiel spoke the word of the Lord to them, the bones came together into skeletons and were covered with flesh. Then life came into the bodies and they stood up, alive again!

Here's what it means: The Israelites had been carried far away from their land and were living in exile in Babylon. They were saying, "Our bones are dried up and our hope is gone" (Ezekiel 37:11 NIV). It was true. They hadn't been listening to the word of the Lord and were spiritually dried up and dead. But God showed them that even though it looked like all hope was gone, He still loved them and was going to do a miracle: They would one day hear and obey God, and He would bring them back to their own land—and He did!

And as I was prophesying, there was a noise, a rattling sound, and the bones came together, bone to bone. I looked, and tendons and flesh appeared on them and skin covered them, but there was no breath in them. Then he said to me, "Prophesy to the breath; prophesy, son of man, and say to it, 'This is what the Sovereign LORD says: Come, breath, from the four winds and breathe into these slain, that they may live.'" So I prophesied as he commanded me, and breath entered them; they came to life and stood up on their feet—a vast army.

EZEKIEL 37:7–10 TNIV

This engraving of Ezekiel's vision of dry bones was made by Gustave Dore around 1870.

WHY DID DANIEL AND HIS FRIENDS REFUSE TO EAT FOOD FROM THE KING'S TABLE?....

The Babylonian official taking care of the four Jewish youths couldn't understand why they wouldn't eat the delicious food prepared by the king's own cooks or drink the best wine in Babylon. Why did they say that the king's food was defiled and choose to eat only vegetables and drink water? There were two good reasons.

First, the Babylonians ate many unclean animals that God had forbidden the Jews to eat. And even clean animals like sheep and cattle had not been slaughtered and bled properly (Leviticus 11; 17:10–14).

Second, the king's food was defiled because the Babylonians worshipped demonic gods, and a portion of the meat and wine was given to the idols, dedicating the entire meal to their idols. Since Daniel and his friends were dedicated to the true God, they didn't want to eat such food.

> But Daniel resolved that he would not defile himself with the king's rich food, or with the wine which he drank; therefore he asked the chief of the eunuchs to allow him not to defile himself. . . . Then Daniel said to the steward whom the chief of the eunuchs had appointed over Daniel, Hananiah, Mishael, and Azariah; "Test your servants for ten days; let us be given vegetables to eat and water to drink."
>
> DANIEL 1:8, 11–12 RSV

Daniel turning down King Nebuchadnezzar's food would be like kids today saying "No thanks" to a pizza buffet. But Daniel knew he was making the right decision.

WHAT DO DANIEL'S VISIONS AND PROPHECIES MEAN?

> "The dream is certain, and its interpretation is sure."
>
> DANIEL 2:45 NKJV

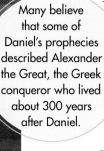

Many believe that some of Daniel's prophecies described Alexander the Great, the Greek conqueror who lived about 300 years after Daniel.

God gave Daniel several dreams, visions, and prophecies, and though each was different, they all described the great empires that would arise in the future. The Babylonian Empire ruled the Middle East during most of Daniel's life. Then came the Persians. The Grecian Empire arose next, and finally the Roman Empire took over.

This is all ancient history now, but in Daniel's day, most of these empires were still in the future. When the prophecies came true, people were amazed that God had accurately described these empires *before* they conquered the world.

Most Christians believe that the book of Daniel also gives a detailed description of the worldwide empire of the Antichrist, which will conquer the entire world during the end times.

HOW DID DANIEL SURVIVE IN A DEN FULL OF LIONS?

> Then the king commanded, and they brought Daniel, and cast him into the den of lions.
>
> DANIEL 6:16 KJV

It wasn't because Daniel was the "lion whisperer." He wasn't. Besides, their keepers made sure that those lions were kept ferociously hungry. As soon as Daniel was pulled up out of the pit, the king commanded that Daniel's *enemies* be thrown in—and before they even reached the floor of the pit, the lions attacked and killed them.

Daniel explained to the king how he had survived the night in the lions' den: "My God sent his angel and shut the lions' mouths" (Daniel 6:22 RSV).

Of course, many Christians in the early church *were* killed by lions in the Roman arena. God could have shut those lions' mouths as well, but He didn't. God knew that the way that the Christian martyrs died, gladly giving up their lives for Jesus' sake, would be a great witness to the Romans who were watching. (See Revelation 12:11.)

DOES GOD STILL SPEAK TO PEOPLE IN DREAMS AND VISIONS?

In the Bible, God often gave people messages or warnings through dreams and visions—and He can still do that today if He chooses. However, it's important to remember that just because you had an unusual dream doesn't mean that God is speaking to you. After all, even dogs dream.

Most of our dreams are jumbled-together bits and pieces of things that we have been thinking about during the day. Often we dream about things we really want (Ecclesiastes 5:3, 7; Isaiah 29:8). It would be a mistake to think that such dreams are a message from God.

Some Christians think that now that the Bible is written, God doesn't speak to believers through dreams and visions anymore. Other Christians believe that God is still perfectly able to give a message that way if He chooses. However, if a message in a dream doesn't line up with what the Bible says, don't pay attention to it.

In the first year of Belshazzar king of Babylon, Daniel had a dream, and visions passed through his mind as he was lying on his bed. He wrote down the substance of his dream.

DANIEL 7:1 NIV

Artist Michael Willmann (1630–1706) painted this picture of Jacob's dream of angels climbing up and down a ladder to heaven. God definitely spoke to people by dreams in Bible times. He can today, too—though we have the Bible now to tell us what He wants us to know.

DID JONAH REALLY SPEND THREE DAYS AND THREE NIGHTS IN THE BELLY OF A GREAT FISH?

> *Now the LORD provided a huge fish to swallow Jonah, and Jonah was in the belly of the fish three days and three nights.*
>
> JONAH 1:17 TNIV

Yes, he did, though it's not certain what kind of fish this was. The Hebrew word in Jonah 1:17 and the Greek word in Matthew 12:40 both mean "great aquatic animal"—so it could have been a sperm whale or a giant white shark—or a whale shark, which can grow up to 50 feet long. All of these giant sea animals have swallowed animals as big as humans.

Another thing, the expression "three days and three nights" can also refer to one whole day and *parts* of two other days. So Jonah didn't necessarily spend a full 72 hours in the sea creature's belly. He could have spent 40 hours—which probably still seemed like forever—and had enough oxygen to survive until the sea creature vomited him up.

Don't forget also that "the LORD had prepared a great fish to swallow up Jonah" (Jonah 1:17 KJV). So even though God used a natural creature, He performed a miracle to make sure Jonah survived the voyage.

Could this be the last thing Jonah saw before he was swalled by the "great fish"?

DOES GOD ACTUALLY CHANGE HIS MIND ABOUT THINGS?

God doesn't change His mind like people do. Some people say one thing, but when they find out the full facts, they change their mind. Or they promise they'll do something, and then change their mind and don't keep their word. God always knows the full facts before He speaks. He always keeps His word.

God says clearly that He will bless people for obeying and punish them for disobeying. However, He *also* says that if a wicked man repents and changes his ways, he will live (Ezekiel 18:1–23). This is because God is a compassionate God and loves to show mercy instead of judgment (Psalm 103:8–10).

God showed mercy to the city of Nineveh when the people there repented. God sent Jonah to Nineveh and told him to warn them that within 40 days Nineveh would be destroyed. Yet when the people turned from their evil ways, God relented—had compassion—and didn't bring the disaster He'd threatened to bring upon them (Jonah 3; see also Exodus 32:1–14).

> *[God] relented and did not bring on them the destruction he had threatened.*
>
> JONAH 3:10 TNIV

WHY DOES GOD SOMETIMES TAKE SO LONG TO ANSWER OUR PRAYERS?..... ➡

Habakkuk once complained, "Oh Lord, how long must I call for help before you listen?" (Habakkuk 1:2 GNT). In the book of Revelation, even the Christian martyrs felt that God was taking a very long time to answer prayer (6:10–11). God told them to wait a little longer and He would answer.

> How long, O LORD, must I call for help, but you do not listen? Or cry out to you, "Violence!" but you do not save? Why do you make me look at injustice? Why do you tolerate wrong? Destruction and violence are before me; there is strife, and conflict abounds.
>
> HABAKKUK 1:2–3 NIV

When we experience a huge problem or an injustice or we feel we just can't stand a situation much longer, we want God to answer our prayers right away. But when He doesn't answer quickly, our patience is tested. And that's one reason why God sometimes makes us wait: to teach us more faith and patience.

God also wants to teach us to be persistent and never give up. That's why Jesus said, "Men always ought to pray and not lose heart" (Luke 18:1 NKJV). In 1 Kings 18:41–45, when God didn't immediately answer Elijah's prayers, the prophet kept praying and praying and praying until God finally did answer.

WILL GOD REFUSE TO BLESS US IF WE DON'T GIVE MONEY TO THE CHURCH?............ ⊘

In Ezra's day, after the Jews started to rebuild God's temple, their enemies forced them to stop (Ezra 3:8–10; 4:23–24). Some 16 years later, the Jews had basically accepted that they would never have a place to worship God. They built their own houses and planted fields and vineyards but no longer tried to rebuild God's house. So God sent a drought to get their attention. The prophet Haggai told the people they had to rebuild the temple if they expected God to bless them.

> *Thus says the LORD of hosts, "Consider your ways! Go up to the mountains, bring wood and rebuild the temple, that I may be pleased with it and be glorified," says the LORD.*
>
> HAGGAI 1:7–8 NASB

In the New Testament, Christians met in homes and had no church buildings, so no one was asked to give to a building fund. The offerings they gave were used to feed and care for the poor (Romans 15:26; 16:3–5).

However, if your family meets in a church building, it is only fair that you contribute something to help build it and keep a roof overhead. God won't necessarily refuse to bless you if you don't, but the Bible does say that He will bless you for giving as much as you're able (2 Corinthians 8:12; 9:6–8).

Many churches hand out envelopes to remind their members to give regularly. And though giving is good, remember that you'll never be able to buy God's love with money—He showed His great love for you by sending Jesus to die on the cross for your sins!

HOW COULD A VIRGIN BECOME PREGNANT?

The Bible clearly states that Mary's fiancé, Joseph, hadn't slept with her yet, so we know that Joseph wasn't Jesus' actual father. We also know that Mary was a virgin and that she hadn't slept with any *other* man, so God did a miracle to get Mary pregnant (Matthew 1:18–20).

We don't really know how He did it. In fact, Mary herself didn't see how it was possible. When the angel told her that she would conceive and give birth to the Son of God, she asked, "How will this be, since I am a virgin?" The angel simply explained, "The Holy Spirit will come on you, and the power of the Most High will overshadow you" (Luke 1:34–35 TNIV).

Since the Holy Spirit is the Spirit of God, and God created all human beings to begin with, He certainly had the power to cause Mary to become pregnant and give birth to baby Jesus.

Then Joseph woke up. He did exactly what God's angel commanded in the dream: He married Mary. But he did not consummate the marriage until she had the baby. He named the baby Jesus.
MATTHEW 1:24–25 MSG

Some think Mary might have been as young as an early teenager when God called her to become the mother of Jesus.

····WHAT DOES iT MEAN TO REPENT?·······

The Bible talks a lot about our need to repent. John the Baptist preached, "Repent, for the kingdom of heaven is at hand!" and Jesus preached, "Repent, and believe in the gospel" (Matthew 3:2; Mark 1:15 NKJV).

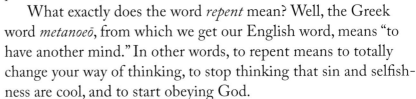

In those days came John the Baptist, preaching in the wilderness of Judaea, and saying, Repent ye: for the kingdom of heaven is at hand.

MATTHEW 3:1–2 KJV

Think of repentance as a U-turn—you're going in one direction (the wrong one) and you completely turn around to the right way!

Later, the apostle Peter also told people to repent (Acts 2:38).

What exactly does the word *repent* mean? Well, the Greek word *metanoeō*, from which we get our English word, means "to have another mind." In other words, to repent means to totally change your way of thinking, to stop thinking that sin and selfishness are cool, and to start obeying God.

The first thing to do when you repent is to believe in the gospel, and when you do that, Jesus' Spirit comes into your life and gives you the power to change your way of thinking. And when you change your old selfish ways and start living a new life, your actions will be the "good fruit" that *shows* that you've had a change of heart (Luke 3:8–14).

WHY DiD JESUS SAY, "iF YOUR RiGHT EYE CAUSES YOU TO SIN, PLUCK iT OUT AND THROW iT AWAY"? ······→

Seems like pirates are always missing an eye for some reason—but probably not because they were following Jesus' advice in Matthew 5:29!

"If your right eye causes you to sin, pluck it out and throw it away; it is better that you lose one of your members than that your whole body be thrown into hell."

MATTHEW 5:29 RSV

If you don't have the willpower to control what you look at, you're going to end up in trouble, because "the lust of the eyes" (1 John 2:16 KJV) is one of the world's biggest problems. For example, guys can't help but notice a beautiful girl pass by. That's not a problem. But if they allow themselves to *desire* her, their minds will fill with lustful thoughts, which might lead to sinful actions.

This applies to other things as well. For example, if a girl desires someone else's iPod, she may begin coveting (lusting for) what belongs to someone else and end up stealing it. That's why the Bible says, "You shall not covet. . .*anything* that belongs to your neighbor" (Exodus 20:17 NIV, emphasis added).

So how do you stop "the lust of the eyes"? Literally gouge them out? No. Jesus was speaking in a parable. David said he had a bridle on his mouth so he wouldn't blurt out the wrong thing (Psalm 39:1). You don't think the king of Israel sat on this throne with a horse's bridle in his mouth, right? In the same way, Jesus' point was that you should do what you have to do to control your eyes. (See also Job 31:1.)

WHAT DID JESUS MEAN WHEN HE SAID, "RESIST NOT EVIL"? ARE WE SUPPOSED TO LET PEOPLE WALK ALL OVER US?.........

> "But I say to you, Do not resist one who is evil. But if any one strikes you on the right cheek, turn to him the other also."
>
> MATTHEW 5:39 RSV

Jesus said, "You have heard that it was said, 'An eye for an eye, and a tooth for a tooth.' But I tell you not to resist an evil person" (Matthew 5:38–39 NKJV). The Law of Moses called for very strict justice: If you were in a fight and someone knocked out your top left tooth, the judges would order his top left tooth knocked out. If he burned you, the officers of the law burned him in the exact same place (Exodus 21:22–25).

Jesus followed His own advice the night He was arrested, allowing the "bad guys" to take Him to an unfair trial and, ultimately, the Crucifixion. But Jesus knew that there was a much bigger purpose to His pain—and He suffered for all of us.

Jesus didn't mean that you shouldn't even defend yourself if someone starts slapping or punching you. You *should* defend yourself. But you shouldn't go looking for a fight. If someone slaps you, don't do the exact same thing back to that person just to get even. "Do not say, 'I'll do to him as he has done to me; I'll pay that man back for what he did'" (Proverbs 24:29 NIV).

Defend yourself, yes, but don't seek revenge. Let God take care of paying someone back. (See Romans 12:17–21.)

DOES JESUS REALLY EXPECT US TO BE PERFECT? ....

> "You, therefore, must be perfect, as your heavenly Father is perfect."
>
> MATTHEW 5:48 RSV

Jesus said, "Be perfect, therefore, as your heavenly Father is perfect" (Matthew 5:48 TNIV). The word *perfect* doesn't mean to be totally without sin. It literally means "complete"—in other words, we are to act completely the way God acts.

Jesus had just finished saying, "Love your enemies" (verse 44). He then went on to explain that even though *we* may have difficulty loving those who mock or hurt us, *God* still loves them. He sends them rain and sunshine as much as He sends these blessings to good people (verse 45).

So if we say that we are God's children, we should act the way that God acts toward our enemies. We should love them and do good things to them.

WHY DID JESUS SAY NOT TO USE "VAIN REPETITIONS" WHEN WE PRAY, YET HE PRAYED THE EXACT SAME WORDS THREE DIFFERENT TIMES?

> "And when you pray, do not keep on babbling like pagans, for they think they will be heard because of their many words."
>
> MATTHEW 6:7 TNIV

Jesus said, "When you pray, do not use vain repetitions as the heathen do. For they think they shall be heard for their many words" (Matthew 6:7 NKJV). Notice that Jesus *didn't* say, "Do not repeat yourself at all." He said, "Do not use *vain* repetitions." Vain means "worthless" or "insincere." His point was that you aren't to keep on repeating words you don't really mean, babbling on and on, just to make your prayer last longer. God isn't impressed by what kind of prayer show you put on.

But if you're really desperate and you're praying with all your heart and not just for show, it's fine if you repeat yourself. Sometimes those are just about the only words you can think of. When

One of the best-known hymns of the church is called "Holy, Holy, Holy," which comes from Isaiah 6. Angels around God's throne repeat those three words all the time—maybe to honor the "Trinity" of God the Father, God the Son, and God the Holy Spirit.

Jesus was in the Garden of Gethsemane, just before He was crucified, He was in such deep agony that He was sweating blood, and He repeated the same prayer three times (Mark 14:32–41; Luke 22:44).

DOES JESUS REALLY WANT US TO BE LIKE THE BIRDS AND NOT WORK AT ALL OR SAVE ANY MONEY, BUT JUST TRUST HIM TO SUPPLY OUR NEEDS?

"Therefore I tell you, do not worry about your life, what you will eat or drink; or about your body, what you will wear. Is not life more important than food, and the body more important than clothes? Look at the birds of the air; they do not sow or reap or store away in barns, and yet your heavenly Father feeds them. Are you not much more valuable than they?"

MATTHEW 6:25–26 TNIV

Who says birds don't work? Sure, if they live in captivity and get their food from a bird feeder, they don't have to search for food. But most birds in the world work hard much of the day. An average bird has to eat its body's weight worth of insects every day, and that means a lot of flying and hunting. And parents feeding growing chicks are on the go from morning to night to find enough food.

God takes care of this cardinal by having a caring human fill a bird feeder. Other birds, in the wild, rely on God in other ways. However they eat, God provides!

Jesus' point was that God provides food for the birds, and because people are worth much more than birds, He will also provide for us. Jesus didn't say, "Do not work." He said, "Do not worry" (Matthew 6:25). We will still have to work for what we get—and like the birds, maybe work hard—but we should trust God and not worry. If we do our part and pray, God will provide our needs.

DO WE ALL HAVE GUARDIAN ANGELS WHO CONSTANTLY WATCH OVER US?

"Watch that you don't treat a single one of these childlike believers arrogantly. You realize, don't you, that their personal angels are constantly in touch with my Father in heaven?"

MATTHEW 18:10 MSG

The Bible tells us that God has put His angels in charge of caring for us and protecting us "in *all* [our] ways" (Psalm 91:11 NKJV). It certainly does sound like His angels are with us all the time, constantly watching over us. But are they the same angels all the time, or is it always a new angel?

Jesus was talking about children when He said, "Do not despise one of these little ones; for I tell you that in heaven their angels always behold the face of my Father who is in heaven" (Matthew 18:10 RSV). Because Jesus said "*their* angels," it sounds like each angel "belongs" to the person he is guarding. That's definitely what the early Christians believed (Acts 12:15).

Many Christians believe that there are one or two angels assigned to each person. This could well be, but we don't know for certain.

Some parents think their kids give guardian angels are real workout! This 1656 painting, by Pietro da Cortona, shows a guardian angel walking a child through danger.

DID JESUS REALLY MEAN IT WHEN HE SAID THAT IF WE BELIEVE WHEN WE PRAY, WE'LL RECEIVE WHATEVER WE PRAY FOR?....

Jesus said, "If you believe, you will receive whatever you ask for in prayer." He also said, "Everything is possible for the person who has faith" (Matthew 21:22; Mark 9:23 GNT). Far too many people pray wishfully, without really expecting that God will answer. They just pray because, well, praying is something that Christians do. When you pray like that, you won't receive anything (James 1:6–7). You need to believe when you pray.

And you need to believe *in God* if you want Him to do something for you. But no matter how much you pray, God won't give you something if it's not His will for you to have it (1 John 5:14–15).

Also, it may not be God's time—yet (Revelation 6:10–11). Sometimes, God's answer is on the way, but the devil is fighting your receiving it (Daniel 10:12–13). So pray and believe. *Keep* praying and believing.

Crossing your fingers and wishing real hard. . .no, that's not what prayer is all about!

But Jesus was matter-of-fact: "Yes—and if you embrace this kingdom life and don't doubt God, you'll not only do minor feats like I did to the fig tree, but also triumph over huge obstacles. This mountain, for instance, you'll tell, 'Go jump in the lake,' and it will jump. Absolutely everything, ranging from small to large, as you make it a part of your believing prayer, gets included as you lay hold of God."

MATTHEW 21:21–22 MSG

ARE WE LIVING IN THE END TIMES?

Christians have different opinions about the end times. Some Christians, called *idealists*, don't believe there will be end times at all; they think the events in Matthew 24 and Revelation symbolize the eternal struggle between good and evil. Others, called *preterists*, believe that Matthew 24

> *Watch therefore: for ye know not what hour your Lord doth come.*
> MATTHEW 24:42 KJV

was fulfilled when the Romans destroyed Jerusalem in AD 70. *Historicists* believe that the events in Matthew 24 and Revelation describe the fall of the Roman Empire and other major events in history.

Christians who believe that the end times are yet to come are called *futurists*—and they have many different ideas about the last days. Some believe that we're already living in the end times. Others believe that the end can begin any day now. Others believe that it's still a ways off.

Some futurists believe that the church has to conquer the world before Jesus can return. Others believe that the world must first conquer the church. As you can see, Christians have many different opinions about the end times.

HOW DID JESUS RISE FROM THE DEAD?

Roman soldiers pass out in terror as Jesus comes back to life, in this painting from the 1500s.

Jesus was definitely dead. He suffered terribly from being beaten and lost so much blood

> *He has risen, just as He said.*
> MATTHEW 28:6 NASB

that, when He was nailed to a cross Friday at noon, He died after only a few hours. His disciples buried Him just before sundown, and Jesus' body lay in a cold tomb Friday evening, all that night, all day Saturday, all Saturday night, and Sunday morning until the sun rose.

Then the Spirit of God did an outstanding miracle and brought Jesus' dead body back to life (Romans 8:11). This was no ordinary miracle. What's more, Jesus wasn't just raised back to life in a normal body as Lazarus had been (John 11:38–44). Jesus was resurrected in an eternal, powerful body—never to die again.

This was such a great miracle that Paul said it was proof that Jesus is the Son of God (Romans 1:3–4).

"I baptize you with water, but he will baptize you with the Holy Spirit."
MARK 1:8 NIV

The Holy Spirit (represented by the dove) fills Jesus' followers at Pentecost (Acts 2:1–4). The flames above each person show the Spirit's baptizing work.

WHAT DOES IT MEAN TO BE BAPTIZED WITH THE HOLY SPIRIT?

John the Baptist said, "I baptize you with water, but he [Jesus] will baptize you with the Holy Spirit" (Mark 1:8 GNT). Christians have two main opinions about what the baptism of the Holy Spirit is.

First, many Christians believe this is talking about salvation—because the moment we accept Jesus as Lord, God sends the Spirit to live in our hearts (Galatians 4:6). Since all Christians must have the Spirit of Christ to be saved (Romans 8:9), they say that being baptized with the Spirit means becoming a Christian.

Other Christians agree that the Holy Spirit "seals" believers (sets God's mark of ownership on them) when they are saved (Ephesians 1:13–14). But they insist that being "baptized with the Holy Spirit" is often a separate event. This is when a believer is filled with the Spirit and speaks in tongues. They point out that, in the Bible, people sometimes received the Holy Spirit after they became Christians (Acts 8:14–17; 19:1–6).

HOW COULD JESUS HAVE NEVER SINNED WHEN THE BIBLE SAYS THAT HE SOMETIMES GOT ANGRY?

Jesus whips the money changers in the temple, in this 1626 painting by the classic artist Rembrandt.

> He looked around at them in anger. . . .
> MARK 3:5 NIV

Many Christians think that it's a sin to become angry, no matter what the reason. So when they read in the Bible that Jesus looked around at the Pharisees with anger, grieved at how hard-hearted they were, they mistakenly imagine that Jesus must have sinned. This is not the case. The Bible says, "If you become angry, do not let your anger lead you into sin" (Ephesians 4:26 GNT). There are sometimes *good* reasons to get angry—like when you see a bully tormenting a smaller kid. But even though you get angry, don't lose control and do something foolish.

WHY DID JESUS IGNORE THE PHOENICIAN WOMAN WHEN SHE BEGGED HIM TO HELP HER?

> Now the woman was a Greek, a Syrophoenician by birth. And she begged him to cast the demon out of her daughter. And he said to her, "Let the children first be fed, for it is not right to take the children's bread and throw it to the dogs."
> MARK 7:26–27 RSV

One day, when Jesus traveled to the region of Tyre, a Phoenician woman, a non-Jew, heard that He was there and repeatedly begged Him to drive a demon out of her daughter (Mark 7:24–30). At first, Jesus ignored the woman. When she persisted, He finally told her that He was "sent only to the lost sheep of Israel." When she continued to beg Him to help her, He said that He couldn't take the children's bread and give it to the dogs (Matthew 15:21–28). Why did He do that?

Jesus loves Gentiles (non-Jews) as much as Jews, but God had specifically promised the Jews that He would send the Savior to them first, and that afterward the Savior would be a blessing to the whole world. God's Son had to care for the children of God (the Jews) before the non-Jews.

Jesus cared for the woman. He was simply taking the gospel *first* "to the lost sheep of Israel" (Matthew 10:5–6 NIV; see also Romans 1:16). But because the woman had such great faith, Jesus eventually responded to her request and healed her daughter.

IS THE DEVIL RESPONSIBLE FOR CAUSING ALL SICKNESS AND DISEASE?

Many Christians think that the devil and his demons are responsible for causing all sicknesses, from the AIDS virus to the common cold. Every time a person is born deaf or blind, they

> "Deaf and dumb spirit, I command you, come out of him and enter him no more!"
>
> MARK 9:25 NKJV

think the devil caused it to happen. This is because the Bible often tells us that Jesus cast out an evil spirit at the same time He healed people's diseases or handicaps (Mark 9:25–26).

Though it is true that evil spirits directly cause *some* illnesses, it's important to remember that there are countless germs and viruses running loose around the world that are perfectly capable of causing sickness all on their own.

Also, many times, Jesus simply healed sickness—from fevers to leprosy—without needing to cast out demons. He healed people because He has power over disease as well as power over demons (Mark 1:29–31, 40–42; 3:1–5; 5:25–29).

Some of the Bible's descriptions of hell sound a bit like the hot lava oozing from a volcano.

IF GOD IS LOVE, WHY WOULD HE SEND SOMEONE TO A PLACE AS HORRIBLE AS HELL?

When Jesus described hell, He used the word *gehenna* and said it was a place "where their worm does not die, and the fire is not quenched" (Mark 9:48 RSV). Therefore, many Christians think that hell is a literal "lake of fire" (Revelation 20:15) where sinners are tormented for all eternity.

However, the name Gehenna comes from the word *ge-hinnom* (the Valley of Hinnom), which was Jerusalem's garbage dump. So hell may be more like a stinky dump.

Many people have difficulty believing that God would let people burn in fire forever. Billy Graham said that he thought that the fire mentioned in the Bible is a burning thirst for God that can never be quenched. He added, "I think that hell. . .is separation from God forever." In other words, people end up separated from God, because that's what they choose—then later they regret their decision forever.

Whether you believe that hell is a lake of fire, a smoking garbage dump, or a lonely separation from God, know this: People *don't have to go there*! Jesus offers us eternal life with God in heaven instead.

> "If your hand or your foot gets in God's way, chop it off and throw it away. You're better off maimed or lame and alive than the proud owner of two hands and two feet, godless in a furnace of eternal fire. And if your eye distracts you from God, pull it out and throw it away. You're better off one-eyed and alive than exercising your twenty-twenty vision from inside the fire of hell."
>
> MARK 9:43–44 MSG

WHY DOES MARK SAY THAT THE WOMEN SAW ONE ANGEL INSIDE JESUS' TOMB, BUT LUKE SAYS THE WOMEN SAW TWO ANGELS THERE? IS THAT A CONTRADICTION?

Early Sunday morning, Mary Magdalene and a group of women went to Jesus' tomb, and to their shock they found that the huge stone blocking the opening of the tomb had been rolled away. The Roman guards were sprawled on the ground unconscious (Matthew 28:1–4). The tomb was like a cave, so the women walked inside to see Jesus' body—but it was missing! Just then they saw an angel who told them that Jesus had risen from the dead (Mark 16:1–7).

Fra Angelico, an artist in the 1400s, went with Mark's description of one angel in Jesus' empty tomb.

Luke tells the same facts, except he says there were *two* angels in the tomb (Luke 24:1–7). Why the difference? Obviously, one of the angels was doing most of the speaking, so he's the only angel Mark mentioned. Luke, who was a stickler for details, mentioned that a second angel was there as well. Often, one Gospel writer includes facts that another writer doesn't mention.

> As they entered the tomb, they saw a young man dressed in a white robe sitting on the right side, and they were alarmed.
>
> MARK 16:5 NIV

WHY DIDN'T JESUS' DISCIPLES BELIEVE AT FIRST THAT HE HAD RISEN FROM THE DEAD?....

Jesus' disciples believed that God could do miracles, but they also knew that Jesus had been killed. John had even watched Jesus die (John 19:33–35). Jesus was dead and buried, so when the women came running, all talking at once, telling the disciples that they'd seen Jesus and that angels had told them Jesus was alive, "they did not believe the women, because their words seemed to them like nonsense" (Luke 24:11 GNT). They thought the women were seeing things.

When the disciples saw Jesus with their own eyes, that's when they finally believed that He was alive. Thomas was the hardest to convince. He thought the other disciples were either hallucinating or seeing Jesus' ghost. But when Jesus showed up again and told Thomas to touch Him and see that He wasn't a ghost, Thomas was convinced too (John 20:24–28).

> Now when Jesus was risen early the first day of the week, he appeared first to Mary Magdalene, out of whom he had cast seven devils. And she went and told them that had been with him, as they mourned and wept. And they, when they had heard that he was alive, and had been seen of her, believed not. After that he appeared in another form unto two of them, as they walked, and went into the country. And they went and told it unto the residue: neither believed they them. Afterward he appeared unto the eleven as they sat at meat, and upbraided them with their unbelief and hardness of heart, because they believed not them which had seen him after he was risen.
>
> MARK 16:9–14 KJV

Have you heard of a "Doubting Thomas"? The nickname comes from one of Jesus' disciples—Thomas—who wouldn't believe Jesus had come back to life unless he could actually touch the nail holes in Jesus' hands and His spear wound!

Nobody knows what they really looked like, but painter Jacob Jordaens imagined Matthew, Mark, Luke, and John like this in the 1600s.

Many have undertaken to draw up an account of the things that have been fulfilled among us, just as they were handed down to us by those who from the first were eyewitnesses and servants of the word. With this in mind, since I myself have carefully investigated everything from the beginning, I too decided to write an orderly account for you, most excellent Theophilus, so that you may know the certainty of the things you have been taught.
LUKE 1:1–4 TNIV

WHY ARE THERE FOUR GOSPELS?

We don't know why God decided that there should be *four* different accounts of Jesus' life, death, and resurrection in the Bible. We can only be glad that there are. Mark tells the entire gospel story quickly in very descriptive, action-packed words, but he skips many interesting parables and stories.

That's where the Gospel of Matthew really shines. It is filled with all kinds of parables, stories, and conversations that Mark left out.

Then Luke researched and wrote his Gospel some years later. He admitted that others had already written about Jesus but still felt that God wanted him to write his version. We're sure glad he did! Luke told many details that both Matthew and Mark left out.

Finally, 60 years after Jesus' resurrection, the apostle John wrote the fourth and final Gospel, and it added a ton of new information about Jesus that we otherwise never would have known.

WHO IS THE HOLY SPIRIT?......→

God is made up of three Persons—God the Father, God the Son (Jesus Christ), and God the Holy Spirit. The Holy Spirit is also called the Spirit of God and the Spirit of Christ (Romans 8:9).

> The angel answered and said to her, "The Holy Spirit will come upon you, and the power of the Most High will overshadow you; and for that reason the holy Child shall be called the Son of God."
>
> LUKE 1:35 NASB

Some people have the idea that the Holy Spirit is just some kind of power or force, some kind of "it," but the Bible makes it clear that the Spirit is a person—and, in fact, is equal in power and wisdom and holiness to God the Father.

The Spirit knows everything that God knows (1 Corinthians 2:10–11). That's why He is also called "the Spirit of truth" (John 16:13).

The Bible describes the Holy Spirit as being "like a dove" (Mark 1:10)—but it doesn't say the Holy Spirit is a dove.

IF JOHN THE BAPTIST TOLD THE ROMAN SOLDIERS TO "DO VIOLENCE TO NO MAN," HOW CAN CHRISTIANS BE POLICE OFFICERS OR SOLDIERS? ↓

The King James Version of the Bible is a good translation, but it is 400 years old, so some of its expressions are a bit unclear today. When John the Baptist told the Roman soldiers, "Do violence to no man" (Luke 3:14 KJV), it was tied to his next two pieces of advice, "Neither accuse any falsely; and be content with your wages."

> Then some soldiers asked him, "And what should we do?" He replied, "Don't extort money and don't accuse people falsely—be content with your pay."
>
> LUKE 3:14 TNIV

The words "Do violence to no man" literally mean "*Do not shake any man.*" In John's day, many Roman soldiers were unhappy with their wages and would "shake down" people and falsely accuse them of crimes to scare them into paying protection money. This is called extortion. In fact, some modern translations, such as Today's New International Version, say: "Don't extort money."

This has nothing to do with soldiers and police officers using necessary force to keep law and order or to defend their country from enemies.

WHY WERE THE PHARISEES SO FOCUSED ON OBEYING TINY LITTLE LAWS?..........

➜

> "But woe to you Pharisees! for you tithe mint and rue and every herb, and neglect justice and the love of God; these you ought to have done, without neglecting the others."
>
> LUKE 11:42 RSV

The Pharisees started out with the right idea. In the past, the Jews had ignored God and disobeyed His law, so the Pharisees decided that they would *always* do their best to obey *every* single rule and commandment. For example, they were so careful to tithe 10 percent of their income that they snipped off one-tenth of tiny garden herbs like mint and rue to give to God.

They got so focused on the tiny details, however, that they lost sight of the big, important commandments, such as loving God and being compassionate toward others (Luke 11:42). They acted holy by praying long prayers in public, but meanwhile they were overcharging poor widows rent (Matthew 6:5; 23:14).

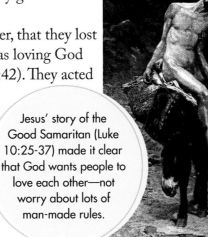

Jesus' story of the Good Samaritan (Luke 10:25-37) made it clear that God wants people to love each other—not worry about lots of man-made rules.

They made sure everyone knew all about it whenever they turned around and gave money to the poor—but because they didn't truly love God and their fellow man, it was all an empty, religious show (Matthew 6:1–2).

WHY WERE THE RELIGIOUS LEADERS OF ISRAEL SO OFFENDED BY WHAT JESUS TAUGHT AND DID?

➜

> The chief priests, the scribes, and the leaders of the people sought to destroy Him.
>
> LUKE 19:47 NKJV

The religious leaders enjoyed their positions of power and authority. They really liked it when people called them "Rabbi" or "Master" and moved aside to give them the most important seats at feasts (Matthew 23:6–7). Their attitude was completely opposite of what Jesus taught—namely, that a good leader should serve the people who were under him (Luke 22:24–26).

Because of their wrong attitude, the religious rulers lost touch with the common people and thus became very jealous when Jesus became popular with the crowds. They became afraid that people would follow Jesus instead of them and they'd lose their positions. They finally became so envious of Jesus that they decided to kill Him (Matthew 27:18).

Another reason they were offended by Jesus was because He constantly broke the little religious laws that were so important to them. They argued, therefore, that He must be a bad person.

Judas betrays Jesus with a kiss—it was a signal to Jesus' enemies indicating who they should arrest.

WHY DID JESUS PICK A DISCIPLE (JUDAS) WHO WOULD BETRAY HIM?.............

Jesus knew that Judas would eventually betray Him and turn Him over to His enemies. So why did He pick Judas as a disciple in the first place? Jesus certainly did not look forward to being beaten, crucified, and killed. He wanted to avoid such a painful death if possible (Matthew 26:38–39).

> That's when Satan entered Judas, the one called Iscariot. He was one of the Twelve.
>
> LUKE 22:3 MSG

However, Jesus knew that it was *not* possible. He had to die to pay the price for our sins. He also knew that the Psalms prophesied that a close friend would be the one to betray Him (Psalm 41:9; John 13:18). Judas was that betrayer.

That didn't mean Judas did a good thing, however. Jesus said, "The Son of Man will die as the Scriptures say he will, but how terrible for that man who will betray the Son of Man!" (Matthew 26:24 GNT).

WHAT KIND OF BODY DID JESUS HAVE AFTER HIS RESURRECTION?................

God raised Jesus up in the same physical body He'd had before. It was the same body, yes—He even had the nail wounds from His crucifixion. But His body was also very different. If Jesus had been brought back to life in His normal body, He eventually would have grown old and died again. God's Spirit not only resurrected Jesus' natural

> Behold my hands and my feet, that it is I myself: handle me, and see; for a spirit hath not flesh and bones, as ye see me have. And when he had thus spoken, he shewed them his hands and his feet.
>
> LUKE 24:39–40 KJV

body, but totally transformed it into a supernatural body (1 Corinthians 15:42–44). Jesus' new, resurrected body was still flesh and bones, but it was now also powerful and eternal.

Sometimes Jesus looked just like the ordinary man His disciples had always known (John 20:24–27), but other times He shone in His full glory. (See Revelation 1:14–16.)

In the beginning was the Word, and the Word was with God, and the Word was God.
JOHN 1:1 KJV

IS JESUS GOD'S SON, OR IS HE GOD HIMSELF?

Jesus is both. He said many times in the Gospels that He was the Son of God and that God was His Father. This is very clear. In fact, God the Father declared, "This is My beloved Son, in whom I am well pleased" (Matthew 3:17 NKJV). But being God's Son doesn't mean that Jesus is *less* than God. Jesus is equal with His Father.

John called Jesus the Word of God and stated, "The Word became a human being" (John 1:14 GNT). But Jesus has always existed, for all eternity, even before He was born on earth. Before the beginning of time, Jesus was already in existence. "In the beginning the Word already existed; the Word was *with* God, and the Word *was* God" (John 1:1 GNT, emphasis added). How could Jesus be God if His Father is God? Well, He's one with His Father (John 10:30).

Isaiah said that the Savior—that's Jesus—would be born as a child but would be called "Mighty God, Everlasting Father, Prince of Peace" (Isaiah 9:6 RSV).

You are not your father. . .and your father is not you. But with God the Father and His Son, Jesus—well, it's different!

WHAT DID JESUS MEAN WHEN HE SAID, "YOU MUST BE BORN AGAIN"?

> Do not be amazed that I said to you, "You must be born again."
>
> JOHN 3:7 NASB

We have all been born physically. That's why our physical bodies are alive in this world. That's the *first* birth. But the spirit that lives inside your body needs to come alive as well. Before God's Holy Spirit enters your life, you're not spiritually alive. That's why Jesus said, "You must be born again" (John 3:7 NASB). He said "again" because spiritual birth is the *second* birth.

Jesus explained, "That which is born of the flesh is flesh, and that which is born of the Spirit is spirit" (John 3:6 NASB). Being "born again" means being "born of the Spirit." This happens when you receive Jesus Christ as your Lord and Savior, and God sends the Spirit into your heart and gives you eternal life. "It is the Spirit who gives life" (John 6:63 NKJV).

WHY ARE THERE SO MANY HYPOCRITES IN THE CHURCH?

> "Stop judging by mere appearances, but instead judge correctly."
>
> JOHN 7:24 TNIV

There *are* hypocrites in church today, of course, just as there were hypocrites in Jesus' day (Matthew 23). Because a hypocrite is someone who's play-acting, pretending to be something they're not, even we—if we're honest—must admit that we are hypocrites at times.

Often, however, when we think someone else is a hypocrite, we're just being quick to judge. For example, if we see a woman dressed in a very nice outfit and wearing expensive rings, we might be tempted to think, *If she were really a Christian, she'd give lots of money to feed the poor!* Yet maybe she *is* giving a great deal to do just that—only we don't *know* about it.

That's why Jesus said, "Do not judge according to appearance, but judge with righteous judgment" (John 7:24 NKJV).

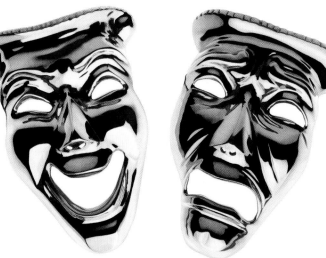

Masks like these are often used to represent the theater—where people pretend to be something they're not!

IS JESUS THE ONLY WAY TO GOD? ⊕

Yes, He is. Jesus said, "I am the way, and the truth, and the life; no one comes to the Father, but by me" (John 14:6 RSV).

Most religions teach some good morals and some truth about God—so you should respect them for that—but that doesn't make them a "way to God." They only have part of the truth and thus can only take people *part way* to God. They can't take anyone all the way, because they can't get across the vast canyon called sin that separates humanity from God.

Jesus is the truth, because everything He taught is true. Jesus is the way, because when He died for your sins, He created a way where there was no way—a bridge across the gap of sin—all the way to God. That's why Jesus is the only one who can save us and give us eternal life. There is no other way to get to heaven.

The early Christians said, "There is salvation in no one else, for there is no other name. . .by which we must be saved" (Acts 4:12 RSV).

> Jesus saith unto him, I am the way, the truth, and the life: no man cometh unto the Father, but by me.
>
> JOHN 14:6 KJV

WHAT DOES THE HOLY SPIRIT DO?

⊕
> But the Comforter, which is the Holy Ghost, whom the Father will send in my name, he shall teach you all things, and bring all things to your remembrance, whatsoever I have said unto you.
>
> JOHN 14:26 KJV

The Holy Spirit does many things. When we believe in Jesus, God sends the Spirit of His Son to dwell in our hearts (Galatians 4:6). We are "born of the Spirit" when this happens (John 3:6). The Holy Spirit then assures us that we belong to God (Romans 8:16).

He helps us to know how to live for God and gives us the power to live as Christians and tell others about Jesus (Acts 1:8). The Spirit also gives us wisdom (Luke 12:11–12) and fills our hearts with love, joy, peace, and hope (Galatians 5:22–23; Romans 15:13). When we feel discouraged, the Holy Spirit, who is also called the Comforter, encourages us (John 16:7).

The Holy Spirit gives us many more wonderful gifts, so ask God to send more of His Holy Spirit into your heart today.

Like the early apostles, modern-day preachers speak in the power of the Holy Spirit. But you don't have to be a preacher to tell others about Jesus— the Holy Spirit will help you, too!

WHY DO CHRISTIANS SUFFER PERSECUTION?..

Jesus said, "If the world hates you, just remember that it has hated me first" (John 15:18 GNT). We know from the Gospels that although many people loved Jesus and obeyed His teachings, He also had enemies who resented what He said and hated what He stood for. Soon they were speaking evil things about Jesus and trying to harm Him physically. That's called persecution.

Jesus warned those who believe in Him, "If people persecuted me, they will persecute you too" (John 15:20 GNT). Being a Christian means living as Jesus lived as much as possible. It means taking a stand for what is right instead of compromising and going along with the crowd. When you do that, people may insult you and avoid you or try to shove you around (Luke 6:22–23).

Many Christians in other countries suffer much more serious persecution than we do. When you are persecuted, remember that Jesus promised to reward us greatly in heaven if we suffer for His sake (Matthew 5:11–12).

> "If the world hates you, you know that it hated Me before it hated you. If you were of the world, the world would love its own. Yet because you are not of the world, but I chose you out of the world, therefore the world hates you. Remember the word that I said to you, 'A servant is not greater than his master.' If they persecuted Me, they will also persecute you. If they kept My word, they will keep yours also. But all these things they will do to you for My name's sake, because they do not know Him who sent Me."
>
> JOHN 15:18–21 NKJV

A man named Stephen was the first Christian killed for following Jesus. You can read the whole story in Acts 6–7.

IF JESUS WAS GOD, WHY DID HE PRAY TO GOD? WASN'T HE JUST TALKING TO HIMSELF?.....

There is one God, but He consists of three different persons—God the Father, God the Son (Jesus), and God the Holy Spirit. The three-in-one God is called the Trinity.

> Holy Father, keep them in thy name, which thou hast given me, that they may be one, even as we are one.
>
> JOHN 17:11 RSV

When Jesus was in heaven before He came to earth, He communicated with His Father all the time, instantly and perfectly. After Jesus became a man, He still spoke with His Father, but now that He had a limited human body, His communication was limited as well. So He prayed using human words. Prayer simply means talking to God.

We talk to God, too, but we definitely can't talk to God the Father on the same level that Jesus could. If you read John 17:1–5, you will see that Jesus talked to the Father as an equal.

The idea of the Trinity has confused people for centuries—but here's one way to explain it: You know how water can be a liquid, a solid (ice), or a gas (steam), like you see in this picture taken near Greenland? God is kind of like that—one God, but in three different "persons."

> Peter replied, "Repent and be baptized, every one of you, in the name of Jesus Christ for the forgiveness of your sins. And you will receive the gift of the Holy Spirit."
>
> **ACTS 2:38** NIV

Men line up to be baptized in the Jordan River—the same water in which Jesus was baptized by John the Baptist.

WHY IS IT SO IMPORTANT TO BE BAPTIZED?

The apostle Peter said, "Repent and be baptized, every one of you, in the name of Jesus Christ for the forgiveness of your sins" (Acts 2:38 NIV). Down through the ages, when people put their faith in Jesus, repented of their sins, and declared that they would follow Jesus, they were baptized in water.

Now, the water doesn't wash away your sins. When Jesus enters your life, His blood cleanses you from sin (1 Peter 3:21; 1 John 1:7). Just the same, it's very important to be baptized. It's an outward declaration that you have had an inward change.

Jesus didn't need to repent of any sins, yet even He allowed John the Baptist to baptize Him, because He wanted to show that it was an important thing to do (Matthew 3:13–15).

ARE CHRISTIANS SUPPOSED TO GIVE UP ALL THEIR MONEY AND WORLDLY POSSESSIONS?

Jesus *does* call some people to give up all their worldly possessions. He told the rich young ruler, "Go, sell everything you have and give to the poor. . . . Then come, follow me" (Mark 10:21 NIV). Many missionaries today give up jobs and possessions in order to preach the gospel.

> All the believers were together and had everything in common. Selling their possessions and goods, they gave to anyone as he had need.
>
> ACTS 2:44–45 NIV

Usually, however, God wants you to start working, in order to earn an honest living for yourself and to be able to help the poor (Ephesians 4:28)—and that includes having money to help support missionaries.

Jesus commanded His disciples to give generously, so when many poor people and widows in Jerusalem became Christians and were in desperate need, wealthy Christians sold their extra lands and houses to raise money for the emergency (Acts 2:44–45). They probably didn't sell the houses they were living in, but they did give generously. Whether we give up everything we own or just a portion of it, we should give generously to God and others.

WHAT DOES IT MEAN TO BELIEVE IN JESUS CHRIST?

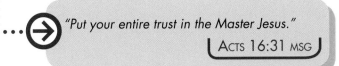

> "Put your entire trust in the Master Jesus."
>
> ACTS 16:31 MSG

The Bible's book of James says even the demons "believe" in God (2:19)—but they're not saved.

When the jailer in Philippi asked, "What must I do to be saved?" Paul answered, "Believe in the Lord Jesus, and you will be saved" (Acts 16:30–31 RSV). Now, surveys show that 88 percent of American adults believe that Jesus Christ was a real person who actually walked the earth. But only 82 percent believe that Jesus is the Son of God and that He died for our sins. So are 88 percent of Americans saved—or is it 82 percent? How many *are* saved? And what exactly does it mean to believe?

The Greek word for believe (*pisteuō*) means "to trust, to rely on, to stick to." It's not enough simply to agree that Jesus exists. It's not even enough to know that He is the Son of God and that He died for our sins. To be saved, you must believe that *you* have sinned and that Jesus died for *your* sins. You must accept Jesus as your Savior and trust Him to save you.

RoMANS← Question & Answer

IS EVERYBODY IN THE WORLD A SINNER—EVEN GOOD, MORAL PEOPLE?

→ For all have sinned, and come short of the glory of God.
ROMANS 3:23 KJV

Many people think that only criminals, drug addicts, or sexually immoral people are sinners because they think that "sin" means only the worst kind of behavior and law-breaking.

But the Greek word for sin (*hamartanō*) means "to err, to miss the mark." So when Romans 3:23 says, "All have sinned and fall short of the glory of God," it's saying that all of us miss the mark and fall short. None of us is perfect. All of us—in big or small ways—have disobeyed God. All of us have done selfish things or hurt others.

So, yes, everybody in the world is a sinner, even moral people who are good *most* of the time. Jesus was the only one who never sinned. That's why only He can save us.

HOW IS SALVATION A FREE GIFT? ↓

Many people have the idea that they have to *earn* their salvation. They figure that if they try to keep the Ten Commandments and do more good deeds than bad deeds, God will reward them for living a (mostly) good life and allow them into heaven.

For the wages of sin is death; but the gift of God is eternal life through Jesus Christ our Lord.
ROMANS 6:23 KJV

But salvation is not like a wage or a reward. You can't earn it. We're all sinners, and "the wages of sin is death" (Romans 3:23; 6:23 KJV). Instead of earning eternal life, we earn death as our "wages."

Fortunately, there is *more* to this verse. The second half reads, "But the gift of God is eternal life through Jesus Christ our Lord." What we could never possibly earn, God will give us for *free* if we simply trust Jesus to save us. Salvation is a gift from a generous, loving God. We can't earn a gift. We can only accept it.

ARE WE SUPPOSED TO SUBMIT TO GOVERNMENTS AND AUTHORITIES EVEN WHEN THEY'RE WRONG? . . . .

When Jesus returns and sets up His kingdom on earth, it will be a perfect government. But until that day, nations will be ruled by imperfect rulers. Some of them govern well, but even

Let every soul be subject unto the higher powers. For there is no power but of God: the powers that be are ordained of God.

ROMANS 13:1 KJV

Some Christians in 1940s Germany felt they had to oppose their government. . . and many of them were killed for standing up to Adolf Hitler and the Nazis.

the best leaders make decisions that cause hardships or suffering. And, sad to say, some governments are run by corrupt, selfish rulers. Most authorities are somewhere in the middle.

Just the same, the Bible tells us, "Be a good citizen. All governments are under God. Insofar as there is peace and order, it's God's order. . . . God also has an interest in keeping order, and he uses them to do it" (Romans 13:1, 4 MSG). According to Paul, there are two main reasons to avoid breaking the law: to avoid being punished by the authorities, and because it's the right way to live.

The only timeS we should not obey a government is if it commands us to do something wrong, deny our faith, or forbids us to tell others about Jesus (Daniel 3:1–18; 6:1–13; Acts 4:18–20).

WERE THERE OUTSTANDING WOMEN IN THE NEW TESTAMENT? . . . .

I commend to you our sister Phoebe. . . .

ROMANS 16:1 NASB

Yes, there were. The Virgin Mary gave birth to the Savior (Luke 1:26–33).

Mary Magdalene helped support Jesus, and she was the first person to see Him after He rose from the dead (Mark 16:9; Luke 8:1–3).

Mary the mother of Mark owned a large house in Jerusalem where many Christians met to pray (Acts 12:11–12).

Priscilla and her husband, Aquila, were Paul's close coworkers. Often when the couple is mentioned, Priscilla's name is mentioned first (Acts 18:1–3, 18; Romans 16:3).

Phoebe, the woman who delivered Paul's letter to the church in Rome, was a deacon of the church of Cenchrea. Paul instructed the Romans, "Assist her in whatever business she has need of you" (Romans 16:1–2 NKJV).

Euodia and Syntyche were Christians in Philippi, and Paul urged the church to "help these women who labored with me in the gospel" (Philippians 4:2–3 NKJV).

My brothers and sisters, some from Chloe's household have informed me that there are quarrels among you. What I mean is this: One of you says, "I follow Paul"; another, "I follow Apollos"; another, "I follow Cephas"; still another, "I follow Christ." Is Christ divided? Was Paul crucified for you? Were you baptized into the name of Paul?

1 CORINTHIANS 1:11–13 TNIV

Christians come from many different backgrounds and worship in different ways—but if Jesus is their focus, they're all on the same team!

CHRISTIANS HAVE MANY DIFFERENT DOCTRINES AND CHURCHES. IS THAT WRONG?

Paul warned Christians against divisions, scolding them because some of them were insisting, "I follow Paul." Others were arguing, "I follow Peter," and others were boasting, "I follow Apollos." Paul asked, "Was Paul crucified for you?" (1 Corinthians 1:12–13 NIV). Of course not. *Jesus* was crucified for us, so we should all follow Jesus.

You should also respect every person who truly follows Jesus, no matter which pastor they prefer to listen to or which church they attend. You might think that your pastor is the best, but it's wrong to think that only the people in your church are true Christians.

You should accept other Christians who have different opinions (Romans 14:1–6). After all, if we agree on the important things about Jesus and the Christian faith, we can be in unity with each other and love each other (Ephesians 4:3–6).

WHEN WE GET TO HEAVEN, WILL WE BE REWARDED FOR OUR GOOD DEEDS AND PUNISHED FOR OUR BAD DEEDS?

> For no other foundation can any one lay than that which is laid, which is Jesus Christ. Now if any one builds on the foundation with gold, silver, precious stones, wood, hay, straw— each man's work will become manifest; for the Day will disclose it, because it will be revealed with fire, and the fire will test what sort of work each one has done. If the work which any man has built on the foundation survives, he will receive a reward. If any man's work is burned up, he will suffer loss, though he himself will be saved, but only as through fire.
>
> 1 CORINTHIANS 3:11–15 RSV

Doing good deeds won't get us into heaven. However, even though we are saved, we will be judged for what we have done. "We must all appear before the judgment seat of Christ, that everyone may receive what is due them. . .whether good or bad" (2 Corinthians 5:10 TNIV). Jesus will reward us for the good we've done, but what about the bad things?

Paul compares our lives to building a house and says that if we build with materials such as gold, silver, and precious stones, when the fire of judgment comes, they won't be affected, and we'll receive a reward.

But if we build with cheap things like wood, hay, and straw, when the fire comes, they'll be burned up. The Bible promises, "If anyone's work is burned, he will suffer loss; but he himself will be saved" (1 Corinthians 3:15 NKJV).

Joseph runs away from his boss's wife, in this 1631 painting by Guido Reni.

WHY DOES THE BIBLE TELL US TO FLEE SEXUAL IMMORALITY?

Some people play around the edges of sexual temptation, enjoying lustful thoughts or looking at pornographic photos, while telling themselves that they'll never actually cross the line and sin

> Flee from sexual immorality. All other sins a man commits are outside his body, but he who sins sexually sins against his own body.
>
> 1 CORINTHIANS 6:18 NIV

sexually. They tell themselves that they're strong enough to resist the actual temptation. But many a young man or woman has been surprised—and ashamed afterward—by how they have given in to temptation in the end.

So don't even get started down that path. Turn away from it. The Bible says: "Do not set foot on the path of the wicked. . . . Avoid it, do not travel on it; turn from it and go on your way" (Proverbs 4:14–15 NIV).

If you find temptation coming out to meet you, flee from it and head the other way (1 Corinthians 6:18). Joseph actually physically ran away when Potiphar's wife tried to tempt him (Genesis 39:11–12).

WHAT IS THE PURPOSE OF COMMUNION?

Jesus celebrated the Lord's Supper (Communion) with His disciples just before He was arrested and crucified, so that's why it's also called the Last Supper. Jesus gave the disciples some bread to eat, telling them that it represented His body that was broken for them. He also gave them wine to drink, which represented His blood poured out for the forgiveness of their sins (Matthew 26:26–28).

Jesus said, "Do this in memory of me" (Luke 22:19 GNT). He wanted His disciples to continue celebrating the Lord's Supper. He said, "This cup is God's new covenant, sealed with my blood. Whenever you drink it, do so in memory of me" (1 Corinthians 11:25 GNT).

Paul explained that every time we take Communion, we're reminding ourselves that Jesus died for us. We are to keep doing this right up until the day that Jesus returns.

> For I have received of the Lord that which also I delivered unto you, that the Lord Jesus the same night in which he was betrayed took bread: And when he had given thanks, he brake it, and said, Take, eat: this is my body, which is broken for you: this do in remembrance of me. After the same manner also he took the cup, when he had supped, saying, this cup is the new testament in my blood: this do ye, as oft as ye drink it, in remembrance of me. For as often as ye eat this bread, and drink this cup, ye do shew the Lord's death till he come.
>
> 1 CORINTHIANS 11:23–26 KJV

WHAT DOES "NEW TESTAMENT" MEAN? ......

In Jesus' day, the Jews called the Law of Moses and the other Scriptures "the Law and the Prophets" (Matthew 7:12 NKJV). These Scriptures talked about the covenant (agreement) that God had made with Israel. The Israelites were His holy, chosen people, and as long as they loved and obeyed Him, God would bless and protect them.

> *After the same manner also he took the cup, when he had supped, saying, this cup is the new testament in my blood: this do ye, as oft as ye drink it, in remembrance of me.*
>
> 1 CORINTHIANS 11:25 KJV

However, the prophet Jeremiah prophesied that one day God would make a "new covenant" with His people (Jeremiah 31:31–33). When Jesus came, He made this covenant by dying on the cross for our sins. At the Last Supper, He offered His disciples a cup of wine, which symbolized His blood, and said, "This cup is the new covenant in My blood" (1 Corinthians 11:25 NKJV).

In the King James Version of the Bible, the words for new covenant are "new testament," so that's why we call the Christian writings the New Testament and the Law and the Prophets the Old Testament.

WHO CAN HAVE AS MUCH LOVE AS THE BIBLE SAYS WE'RE SUPPOSED TO HAVE? ISN'T THAT UNREALISTIC? ......

The kind of love Paul describes in 1 Corinthians 13 is so great that you might think that ordinary people will never be able to set aside all their anger, jealousy, and prejudices and have that kind of love.

Well, you might not have that much love at the beginning, but as you grow in your Christian faith, you become more loving. You get love by yielding your heart to God. It helps to read 1 Corinthians 13 often. Showing love to other people is one of the proofs that you have

> Here's the ultimate example of love: "But God demonstrates his own love for us in this: While we were still sinners, Christ died for us" (ROMANS 5:8 NIV).

127

God's Spirit in your life (Galatians 5:22). "God's love has been poured into our hearts through the Holy Spirit which has been given to us" (Romans 5:5 RSV). So pray for God to give you more love.

→ *Love is patient, love is kind and is not jealous; love does not brag and is not arrogant, does not act unbecomingly; it does not seek its own, is not provoked, does not take into account a wrong suffered, does not rejoice in unrighteousness, but rejoices with the truth; bears all things, believes all things, hopes all things, endures all things. Love never fails.*

1 CORINTHIANS 13:4–8 NASB

WHAT DOES THE BIBLE MEAN WHEN IT SAYS THAT WE WILL BE RESURRECTED?

Some people think that Jesus saves just their *spirit*, so when their body dies, they leave it behind forever and just their spirit lives eternally in heaven. They guess that it sort of floats around on clouds forever because it is just a spirit, after all.

Christians' spirits *do* go to heaven at first, but God has a long-range plan: He wants to save your physical body, too, and reunite it with your spirit. To do this He will resurrect your body. To resurrect means to bring back to life. For your body to live forever, God must *change* it to make it powerful and indestructible and eternal—just like Jesus' resurrection body (Philippians 3:20–21; 1 John 3:2).

The resurrection will happen at the very end of time when Jesus returns (1 Thessalonians 4:14–17). To learn more, read 1 Corinthians chapter 15.

→ *But now is Christ risen from the dead, and become the firstfruits of them that slept. For since by man came death, by man came also the resurrection of the dead. For as in Adam all die, even so in Christ shall all be made alive. But every man in his own order: Christ the firstfruits; afterward they that are Christ's at his coming.*

1 CORINTHIANS 15:20–23 KJV

Your resurrection body will be something like the butterfly is to the caterpillar that first spun its cocoon—still you, but better, freer, more beautiful!

WHY WAS THE APOSTLE PAUL BEATEN UP SO MUCH?.......⬇

Paul said, "Anyone who wants to live all out for Christ is in for a lot of trouble; there's no getting around it" (2 Timothy 3:12 MSG). Paul definitely lived all out

> *What they did to Jesus, they do to us—trial and torture, mockery and murder. . . .*
> 2 CORINTHIANS 4:10 MSG

for Christ. He preached the gospel boldly and very publicly in many cities, so he had many opportunities to lead people to faith in Jesus Christ.

Paul's first rough encounter was with Jesus Himself—on the road to Damascus. Read the whole story in Acts 9:1–19.

This also meant, however, that he had a greater-than-average amount of run-ins with religious people who hated his message. These enemies didn't want to lose control over the people, so they tried to stop Paul from preaching the gospel. Sometimes they beat Paul themselves; sometimes they talked gangs of thugs into doing it; other times they got the city rulers to do it (Acts 14:19; 16:16–24; 17:5).

WHAT DOES IT MEAN NOT TO BE UNEQUALLY YOKED WITH UNBELIEVERS?...............⬇

In the Old Testament, God commanded the Jews, "Do not plow with an ox and donkey yoked together" (Deuteronomy 22:10 NIV). They're un-equal. The ox is larger and stronger and takes big-

> *Do not be yoked together with unbelievers.*
> 2 CORINTHIANS 6:14 NIV

ger steps, and the donkey can't keep up. The ox pulls the plow one direction while the donkey pulls it another, and they can barely plow a straight line. It doesn't make sense to expect them to work well together.

In the same way, Paul said that it just doesn't work when a Christian and an unbeliever are together in a close relationship. Unbelievers think and live differently from the way a Christian thinks and lives, and they'll end up pulling you off track.

Of course, you can be friends with someone who isn't a Christian, but your closest friends should be people who share your faith and values.

HOW CAN WE BE SONS AND DAUGHTERS OF GOD? ISN'T JESUS GOD'S ONE AND ONLY SON?..... ⊍

The Bible tells us that Jesus is God's "one and only Son" (John 3:16 NIV). However, God also says to believers, "I will be a father to you,

Adoption brings a non-related person into a family—and gives her an official, permanent place!

> "I will be a Father to you, and you will be my sons and daughters, says the Lord Almighty."
>
> 2 CORINTHIANS 6:18 NIV

and you shall be sons and daughters to Me" (2 Corinthians 6:18 NASB). How can this be?

Well, Jesus is God's only *natural* Son—made of the same substance as God the Father, and equal with God—but God loved us so much that once Jesus Christ died for our sins, God forgave us and *adopted* us. We weren't His natural children, but He adopted us as His sons and daughters and sent His Spirit to live in our hearts. That's why we can call God our Father (Romans 8:15; Galatians 4:4–6).

WHAT WAS PAUL'S "THORN IN THE FLESH"?..... ⊍

Paul said that God gave him a "thorn in the flesh" (2 Corinthians 12:7 KJV) that he couldn't get rid of. Most Bible scholars believe that this was a long-lasting illness or disability that God used to keep Paul humble. It wasn't an actual thorn that had worked its way into Paul's flesh.

> In order to keep me from becoming conceited, I was given a thorn in my flesh, a messenger of Satan, to torment me.
>
> 2 CORINTHIANS 12:7 TNIV

Most likely it was some kind of eye disease, because Paul complained that his sight was so bad that he had to write in very large letters. He also said that the Christians in Galatia loved him so much that they gladly would have plucked out their own eyes and given them to him if it would have helped (Galatians 4:15; 6:11). Whatever this illness was, Paul had it his whole life.

This close-up of a rose stem shows a lot of sharp thorns. Real thorns probably weren't Paul's problem, but you can imagine how much his problem hurt.

WHY DID PAUL WRITE SO MUCH ABOUT TRUSTING IN JESUS INSTEAD OF RELIGIOUSLY TRYING TO OBEY THE LAW OF MOSES?....

Until Jesus came, the Law of Moses was all the Jews had to teach them how to live as God's people. They tried very hard to keep all its commandments because they thought that's how they could earn eternal life (John 5:39).

When they sinned, they had to sacrifice an animal, and the blood covered their sins. The problem was that such sacrifices couldn't permanently forgive their sins. When Jesus died on the cross and poured out His blood, all people had to do was to believe in Him and all their sins would be forgiven and they'd have eternal life (Hebrews 10:11–14).

> O foolish Galatians! Who has bewitched you, before whose eyes Jesus Christ was publicly portrayed as crucified? Let me ask you only this: Did you receive the Spirit by works of the law, or by hearing with faith?
>
> GALATIANS 3:1–2 RSV

However, some Jewish teachers insisted that people still had to keep the Law of Moses to be saved (Acts 15:1). These teachers went to the churches in Galatia and confused the new Christians, so Paul made it very clear that just believing in Jesus was enough for salvation.

Hebrews 3 describes Jesus as being greater than Moses—who came back from heaven to see Jesus' transfiguration. Read the whole story in Matthew 17:1–8.

131

WHAT IS GRACE? ↓

Grace means several things in the New Testament.

> For it is by grace you have been saved, through faith—and this is not from yourselves, it is the gift of God.
>
> EPHESIANS 2:8 TNIV

When we say that someone is "gracious" or "full of grace," we mean that they are good, kind, and merciful. This is what John meant when he said that Jesus was "full of grace and truth" (John 1:14 KJV).

In New Testament times, *grace* also meant the kindness and mercy of a master toward a servant. The Bible says, "By grace you have been saved through faith, and that not of yourselves; it is the gift of God" (Ephesians 2:8 NKJV). We have been saved from hell by God's kindness and mercy. He doesn't expect us to work for eternal life or to do enough good deeds to earn such a reward. We couldn't earn eternal life no matter how hard we worked, so God graciously gave us salvation free, as a gift.

We say a good figure skater is "graceful"—smooth in movement and pleasing to watch. That's one definition of the word, but not the one the Bible uses.

← HOW SHOULD CHILDREN TREAT THEIR PARENTS?

> Children, obey your parents in the Lord, for this is right. Honor your father and mother (which is the first commandment with a promise), so that it may be well with you, and that you may live long on the earth. Fathers, do not provoke your children to anger, but bring them up in the discipline and instruction of the Lord.
>
> EPHESIANS 6:1–4 NASB

The fifth commandment reads: "Honor your father and your mother" (Exodus 20:12 NIV). In the New Testament, Paul writes, "Children, obey your parents in the Lord, for this is right" (Ephesians 6:1 NIV).

Parents not only care for their kids physically; they also teach them about the Lord. If children don't honor their father and mother, they definitely won't honor the invisible God their parents are teaching them about. John writes, "If any one says, 'I love God,' and hates his brother [or his parents], he is a liar; for he who does not love his brother [or his parents] whom he has seen, cannot love God whom he has not seen" (1 John 4:20 RSV).

Loving and honoring and obeying go hand in hand. If you love your parents, you will honor and obey them; children who honor their parents are taking the first step toward loving and obeying God.

WHAT IS THE ARMOR OF GOD?

The early Christians were familiar with the armor that Roman soldiers wore. It was quite impressive-looking and very effective in protecting the soldiers from their enemies. Paul explained that Christians have a spiritual enemy who hates us—the devil—and we need to cover our bodies with *spiritual* armor.

Just as a Roman soldier had a breastplate—iron armor covering his chest and stomach—we need Christ's righteousness to cover our hearts. We need the helmet of salvation protecting our heads and the shield of faith to stop the flaming arrows of the devil from hitting and wounding us.

We also need the belt of truth, the sword of the Spirit (the Word of God) with which to attack the enemy, and sturdy shoes so we are ready to preach the gospel. We can't skip one piece of armor. Paul said twice to "put on the *full* armor of God."

Put on the whole armour of God, that ye may be able to stand against the wiles of the devil. For we wrestle not against flesh and blood, but against principalities, against powers, against the rulers of the darkness of this world, against spiritual wickedness in high places. Wherefore take unto you the whole armour of God, that ye may be able to withstand in the evil day, and having done all, to stand. Stand therefore, having your loins girt about with truth, and having on the breastplate of righteousness; and your feet shod with the preparation of the gospel of peace; above all, taking the shield of faith, wherewith ye shall be able to quench all the fiery darts of the wicked. And take the helmet of salvation, and the sword of the Spirit, which is the word of God.

EPHESIANS 6:11–17 KJV

WHY WAS PAUL IN PRISON? →

My imprisonment here has had the opposite of its intended effect.

PHILIPPIANS 1:12 MSG

When Paul visited Jerusalem to take money to the poor Christians there, he was attacked by religious enemies and arrested by the Romans. The Roman governor, Felix, would have released Paul if he had paid a bribe, but Paul refused to do that. Paul knew that God wanted him to go to Rome to preach the gospel to the emperor and his court. (See Acts 21:27–34; 23:11; 24:26.)

At first other Christians thought it was a huge defeat that Paul was in prison, but Paul said, "I want you to know, my friends, that the things that have happened to me have really helped the progress of the gospel" (Philippians 1:12 GNT).

After Paul preached in Rome, it appears he was released from prison and was free to travel to Spain to preach the gospel there as well (Romans 15:24, 28).

DID JESUS GIVE UP HIS POWER AS GOD WHEN HE CAME TO EARTH?..... →

Who, being in very nature God, did not consider equality with God something to be grasped, but made himself nothing. . . .

PHILIPPIANS 2:6–7 NIV

"Though he was in the form of God. . .[Jesus] emptied himself, taking the form of a servant, being born in the likeness of men" (Philippians 2:6–7 RSV). When Jesus was born as a baby in a limited, mortal human body, that body simply couldn't contain all the power and glory of God.

Jesus didn't stop being God. He didn't stop being the Son of God. But He had to set aside most of His divine power. He had to "empty himself" of much of the glory that He'd had when He was with His Father in heaven (John 17:5).

Once Jesus was raised from the dead in a powerful, eternal body, however, He was once again able to contain all the power of God. After Jesus' resurrection, "his eyes were like blazing fire. His feet were like bronze glowing in a furnace, and his voice was like the sound of rushing waters" (Revelation 1:13–15 NIV).

It's hard to be more powerless than a newborn baby—which is exactly how Jesus came to earth!

HOW IS JESUS CHRIST DIFFERENT FROM EVERY OTHER FAMOUS MAN WHO STARTED A RELIGION?.....

Every religious leader who has ever lived has claimed to have some new revelation from God, or has preached a new set of commandments that, if you will obey them, will supposedly make you good enough to go to heaven. Some, like Confucius, simply taught morals to make people better citizens. And one after another, all of these religious leaders died. They were mere men who could not give eternal life, even to themselves. Jesus was not just a man, "for by him all things were created" (Colossians 1:16 NIV). That means that He was God who created the heavens and the earth in the beginning (Genesis 1:1). When Jesus was on earth, He was God in the body of a human being (John 1:1, 14).

Though Jesus' enemies killed His physical body, He only allowed that so He could pay the price for our sins. When His work was finished, Jesus was raised back to life by the Spirit of God, never to die again. No other religious teacher has come even close to doing any of these things.

> He is the image of the invisible God, the first-born of all creation; for in him all things were created, in heaven and on earth, visible and invisible, whether thrones or dominions or principalities or authorities—all things were created through him and for him.
>
> COLOSSIANS 1:15–16 RSV

This statue of Confucius stands near a lake in Yueyang, China.

HOW COME SATAN IS ALLOWED TO HINDER GOD'S PLANS?.......

For we wanted to come to you—certainly I, Paul, did, again and again—but Satan stopped us.

1 THESSALONIANS 2:18 NIV

The devil is powerful, but not more powerful than God. And one day, it will be God's angels who defeat Satan and his demons (see Revelation 12:7–8).

Paul told the Christians in Thessalonica, "We wanted to come to you—even I, Paul, time and again—but Satan hindered us" (1 Thessalonians 2:18 NKJV). The Greek word translated "hinder" means "to cut in, to interrupt." Satan fought God's plans very hard. He cut in and tried to block Paul, like a bully cutting in front of him on a racetrack to bump him off course or slow him down.

Satan didn't fight only Paul, however. He has been fighting all of God's people for centuries, including us today.

Why does God allow Satan to cause so much trouble in the world? There are many reasons. First, God allows Satan to test us so that we will come out stronger. God is able also to bring good out of the evil Satan tries to do (Genesis 50:20; Romans 8:28).

However, God doesn't give us a full explanation to this question. He *does*, however, warn us to be alert to the fact that the devil is out to fight and destroy us (1 Peter 5:8). That's why we need to pray and stay close to Jesus.

WHAT IS THE RAPTURE?.........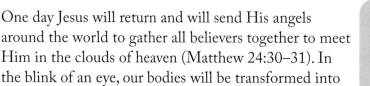

Then we which are alive and remain shall be caught up together with them in the clouds.

1 THESSALONIANS 4:17 KJV

One day Jesus will return and will send His angels around the world to gather all believers together to meet Him in the clouds of heaven (Matthew 24:30–31). In the blink of an eye, our bodies will be transformed into supernatural, eternal bodies.

Being "caught up together. . .in the clouds" (1 Thessalonians 4:17 NIV) is called the Rapture. *Rapture* comes from the Latin word *rapere*, which means "to seize." It describes the angels seizing and snatching us up from the earth.

Some people spend a lot of time trying to figure out when the Rapture will happen, but they can only guess. Jesus said that nobody except for God knows the day or the hour that He will return. Even the angels who will be doing the actual snatching don't know when the Rapture will happen (Matthew 24:36).

IS IT WRONG TO BE RICH?......→

> Lust for money brings trouble and nothing but trouble.
> 1 Timothy 6:9 MSG

It is wrong to be rich if you *become* rich by cheating people and taking advantage of the laborers working for you (James 5:1–6). Unfortunately, this is how many selfish people become wealthy. David once confessed that he was envious of the rich oppressors—until God showed him how they would come to a terrible end (Psalm 73:3–20). Paul warns Christians not to love money and says that those who desire to be rich end up straying from the faith (1 Timothy 6:9).

Yet money itself is not evil. Many good Christians have become wealthy through honest business practices; they pay fair wages to their employees; they give generously to help spread the gospel, and they donate to charities that help the poor. Paul advised rich Christians to be "rich in good works, ready to give, willing to share" (1 Timothy 6:17–18 NKJV). As long as they're doing that, there's nothing wrong with their wealth.

WHAT DOES IT MEAN THAT THE BIBLE IS INSPIRED BY GOD?

> All Scripture is God-breathed and is useful for teaching, rebuking, correcting and training in righteousness.
> 2 Timothy 3:16 TNIV

Older Bible translations say, "All scripture is given by inspiration of God" (2 Timothy 3:16 KJV). That already tells us a lot—that the entire Bible was thought up by God.

But the meaning of the verse goes even deeper. The verse literally means "All scripture is God-breathed." The Bible was not just an idea that God had something to do with. Rather, the Word of God came from God's own mouth. God spoke it and breathed it out.

An angel whispers God's words into the ear of the Gospel writer Matthew, in a painting by the famous artist Rembrandt.

Most of the time, God's Spirit filled godly men and women and used their mouths to speak His words. "For prophecy never came by the will of man, but holy men of God spoke as they were moved by the Holy Spirit" (2 Peter 1:21 NKJV). In New Testament times, God's Spirit filled the minds of the apostles and told them what to write.

*A man that is an heretick after the first
and second admonition reject.*
TITUS 3:10 KJV

WHAT IS HERESY?

These days, we normally understand *heresy* to mean "false teaching," and that's what it does mean. Originally, however, a heresy meant a "choice" or a "sect."

A heresy wasn't just a Christian's harmless opinion of what a verse meant. It was a choice to believe something false, something that was different from the plain, clear teaching of the Bible. A heretic was an opinionated person who chose to follow his own divisive ideas even if he had to twist Scripture to make it line up with his opinions.

Paul described heretics as "savage wolves" tearing apart the flock. He warned the church, "From among yourselves men will rise up, speaking perverse things, to draw away the disciples after themselves" (Acts 20:29–30 NKJV).

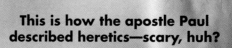

**This is how the apostle Paul
described heretics—scary, huh?**

IN THE BIBLE, A CHRISTIAN NAMED PHILEMON OWNED A SLAVE. DOES THAT MEAN GOD APPROVES OF SLAVERY?......→

There were slaves in Old Testament times, and God put up with man-made customs for quite a while, because people were too hard-hearted to change (Matthew 19:3–8). Nevertheless, foreign slaves who ran away from their masters and made it to Israel automatically became free people (Deuteronomy 23:15–16).

There were millions of slaves in the Roman Empire, and if Paul had insisted that all slaves be freed, he would have had to stop preaching the gospel to start leading an armed slave revolt—and the church would have been crushed. So Paul advised slaves to seek their freedom if they could, but to be content if they couldn't (1 Corinthians 7:21). He told masters to treat their slaves well, knowing that they, too, had a Master in heaven (Colossians 4:1).

Nevertheless, when writing to a friend who owned a slave, Paul told the master to receive the slave "no longer as a slave but more than a slave—a beloved brother" (Philemon 16 NKJV). Centuries later, Christians acted on this very principle and pushed to free all slaves.

Perhaps the reason he was separated from you for a little while was that you might have him back for good—no longer as a slave, but better than a slave, as a dear brother. He is very dear to me but even dearer to you, both as a man and as a brother in the Lord.

PHILEMON 15–16 NIV

Christians were a strong force in ending slavery in England and the United States.

WHAT DO ANGELS DO?

One of the angels' main jobs is to guard human beings. This is why people call them "guardian angels" (see Psalm 91:11). They sometimes rescue people in trouble (Genesis 19:4–16; Acts 5:17–25) and bring God's judgment on the disobedient (2 Samuel 24:13–16).

However, angels do much more than that. They also carry important messages to people (Matthew 1:20–21; Acts 27:23–24), and they spend a great deal of time praising God and His Son, Jesus (Revelation 5:11–12).

God also sends angels to minister to Christians (Hebrews 1:14). To "minister to" means to serve or care for. For example, after the devil had tempted Jesus, angels came and ministered to Him; and when Jesus was praying desperately in the Garden of Gethsemane, an angel strengthened Him (Matthew 4:11; Luke 22:42–44).

> And did he ever say anything like this to an angel? Sit alongside me here on my throne until I make your enemies a stool for your feet. Isn't it obvious that all angels are sent to help out with those lined up to receive salvation?
> HEBREWS 1:13–14 MSG

An angel comforts Jesus the night before His arrest, in a 19th-century painting by Carl Bloch.

WHAT DOES IT MEAN TO HARDEN YOUR HEART?

> *While it is said, To day if ye will hear his voice, harden not your hearts, as in the provocation.*
>
> HEBREWS 3:15 KJV

God wants His people to hear what He says and to receive His Word in their hearts (Deuteronomy 6:6). That's why Jesus described God's Word as a seed of grain and people's hearts as soil. He said some soil was rocky, some was trampled down hard, some was choked with thorns, but some was soft "good earth"—the kind of heart where God's Word will grow and bring forth a good crop (Matthew 13:3–8, 18–23).

David says in the Psalms, "Today, if you would hear His voice, do not harden your hearts" (Psalm 95:7–8 NASB; see also Hebrews 3:15). Don't make your heart as hard as solid, dry earth so that the Word of God can't even enter in and grow. Keep your heart soft and ready to receive.

WHY DOES GOD ALLOW US TO GO THROUGH HARD TIMES?........

> *And have you forgotten the exhortation which addresses you as sons?—"My son, do not regard lightly the discipline of the Lord, nor lose courage when you are punished by him. For the Lord disciplines him whom he loves, and chastises every son whom he receives."*
>
> HEBREWS 12:5–6 RSV

Christians have wondered this for the past 2,000 years: "If God loves me so much that He sent His own Son to die for my sins, why does He let me go through hard times? Why does He take so long to answer my prayers when I need His help?"

Well, God sends hardship precisely because He *does* love you! God allows you to endure difficulties, because that is His way of disciplining and training you. Think of an athlete with a no-nonsense trainer who puts him on a strict diet and has him go through long, repetitive workouts to build up muscles and speed.

For Christians, God's discipline produces righteousness, peace, and holiness (Hebrews 12:10–11). It also teaches us patience.

So cheer up! Tough times are *proof* that God loves you! "No discipline seems pleasant at the time, but painful" (Hebrews 12:11 NIV), but "do not lose heart when he rebukes you, because the Lord disciplines those he loves" (Hebrews 12:5–6 NIV).

Hard things can make us stronger!

WHY DOES JAMES SAY THAT SIMPLY BELIEVING IN GOD IS NOT ENOUGH? DOESN'T THIS CONTRADICT WHAT PAUL TAUGHT?

Paul said, "Believe in the Lord Jesus, and you will be saved" (Acts 16:31 RSV). Paul also said that God's grace alone saves us, without our doing any good works or good deeds (Romans 10:9–10). Yet James said, "What does it profit, my brethren, if someone says he has faith but does not have works. Can faith save him?. . . Faith by itself, if it does not have works, is dead" (James 2:14, 17 NKJV).

There's no contradiction here, despite how it might seem. When you truly believe in Jesus, you naturally want to obey Him (1 John 5:1–3). You make Him the center of your life. When Jesus is the center of your life, you will naturally do good works and good deeds. "Our love should not just be words and talk; it must be true love, which shows itself in action" (1 John 3:18 GNT).

So, although good deeds can't save you, if you have true faith, your faith will cause you to do good works. That's the proof that you have genuine faith.

Martin Luther, a great Christian leader from the 1500s, wondered if the book of James should even be part of the Bible—because he thought it contradicted salvation by faith. But James was really just saying that true faith leads to good works.

What use is it, my brethren, if someone says he has faith but he has no works? Can that faith save him?
JAMES 2:14 NASB

DO YOU NEED TO BE BAPTIZED IN ORDER TO BE SAVED?

> This water symbolizes baptism that now saves you. . . .
>
> 1 PETER 3:21 NIV

Peter said, "Repent and be baptized. . .in the name of Jesus Christ for the forgiveness of your sins" (Acts 2:38 TNIV).

Some Christians therefore believe that unless you are baptized, you are not saved.

However, Peter later compared baptism and salvation to Noah and his family being safe on the ark and talked about them being "brought safely through the water." Then he added, "Corresponding to that, baptism now saves you—not the removal of dirt from the flesh, but an appeal to God for a good conscience" (1 Peter 3:20–21 NASB).

The water doesn't wash away your sins. Jesus' blood is what cleanses your sins and washes your guilty conscience (1 John 1:7). Just the same, it's very important to be baptized as a symbol of your salvation.

Jesus told a thief, dying on a cross beside Him, "Today, you will be with me in paradise" (Luke 23:43)—but there's nothing in the Bible about that thief being baptized!

HOW CAN WE BE SURE THAT THE STORIES ABOUT JESUS ARE TRUE?

> We have not followed cunningly devised fables. . . .
>
> 2 PETER 1:16 KJV

About 30 years after Jesus' crucifixion and resurrection, the apostle Peter said, "We have not followed cunningly devised fables, when we made known unto you the power and coming of our Lord Jesus Christ, but were eyewitnesses of his majesty" (2 Peter 1:16 KJV).

The Greek Christians had grown up hearing fables about the so-called Greek gods—Zeus, Hercules, Hades, and others. They knew that those stories were definitely made up. Peter said that Jesus was different. He was a real person who had actually lived, and Peter and the other disciples had seen Him.

About 60 years after Jesus' crucifixion, the apostle John, who was also an eyewitness to those events, wrote a Gospel (John 19:33–35; 21:24). John declared that he and the other disciples had heard Jesus, seen Him with their own eyes, and even touched Him—so they knew good and well that Jesus was real and that He actually did and said the things that the Gospels say He did and said (1 John 1:1).

GOD LOVES THE WORLD, AND WE ARE TOLD TO iMiTATE GOD. WHY THEN ARE WE WARNED NOT TO LOVE THE WORLD?.........→

God loved the world *so much* that He sent His only Son to die on the cross, so that whoever believes in Jesus can have eternal life (John 3:16). We are told to love just like God loves. Yet in a later letter, John says, "If anyone loves the world, the love of the Father is not in him" (1 John 2:15 NKJV). Which of these statements is true?

> Do not love the world or the things in the world. If anyone loves the world, the love of the Father is not in him. For all that is in the world—the lust of the flesh, the lust of the eyes, and the pride of life—is not of the Father but is of the world. And the world is passing away, and the lust of it; but he who does the will of God abides forever.
>
> 1 JOHN 2:15–17 NKJV

They both are. When John said that "God so loved the world," he was talking about the *people* in the world. We are to love people—our fellow human beings. However, Jesus *didn't* love the power and riches and glory of the world's kingdoms. When Satan offered these things to Him, Jesus refused (Matthew 4:8–10).

We are to love people as much as we love our own selves, but we are not to love the riches and power and human glory that the world offers.

→ Here's another way to "love the world"—taking care of its natural resources. What God doesn't want you to love is the sinful ways the world works.

WHAT DOES THE WORD ANTICHRIST MEAN?

Here's how you test for the genuine Spirit of God. Everyone who confesses openly his faith in Jesus Christ—the Son of God, who came as an actual flesh-and-blood person—comes from God and belongs to God. And everyone who refuses to confess faith in Jesus has nothing in common with God. This is the spirit of antichrist that you heard was coming. Well, here it is, sooner than we thought!

1 JOHN 4:2–3 MSG

The devil whispers into the Antichrist's ear, in a painting from the early 1500s.

Antichrist means "against Christ." A person who is *antichrist* knows what Jesus stands for yet hates Him and fights against Him. Sometimes people who *say* they love Jesus are actually against Him, because they teach lies about Him or deny some of the basic truths of the gospel.

When John talks in this verse about people being antichrist, he means people who deny that Jesus lived on earth in a human body (1 John 4:2–3).

Christians also believe that there will be one final world dictator called the Antichrist in the end times, because John wrote, "It is the last hour; and as you have heard that the Antichrist is coming, even now many antichrists have come" (1 John 2:18 NKJV). This Antichrist is also called "the man of sin" and "the beast" (2 Thessalonians 2:3–4; Revelation 13).

WHO WERE THE GNOSTICS?

In John's day, a false teaching arose in the church. Many Greeks believed that all physical things were evil—rocks, trees, air, water, and human bodies. Only spiritual things were good. They thought that man's "good spirit" was trapped in his "evil body," so dying was a good thing.

Little children, it is the last time: and as ye have heard that anti-christ shall come, even now are there many antichrists; whereby we know that it is the last time.

1 JOHN 2:18 KJV

These Greeks liked Jesus' message of love and brotherhood, but they couldn't believe that such a good Savior would come to earth in an "evil body." They therefore said that Jesus *appeared* to have a body, but He'd really only been a spirit. These teachers were called Gnostics.

John argued that he had not only seen and heard Jesus, but even *touched* Him (1 John 1:1). John had a blunt warning to the Gnostics: He said that anyone who admitted that Jesus Christ came in the flesh as a human being was of God, but that anyone who denied this was not saved (1 John 4:2–3).

HOW CAN WE KNOW WHEN SOMEONE IS A FALSE TEACHER?

Jesus said to "beware of false prophets." Even if they speak pretty and wise-sounding words, what their words lead people to believe and do is what matters (Matthew 7:15–20). Some corrupt teachers teach that you can live as you please and sin all you want, that it's no big deal to God and He'll quickly forgive you (2 Peter 2:18–19). Those kinds of false teachers are obvious, but some are less easy to spot.

> For certain men have crept in unnoticed, who long ago were marked out for this condemnation, ungodly men, who turn the grace of our God into lewdness and deny the only Lord God and our Lord Jesus Christ.
>
> JUDE 4 NKJV

Others might teach that you have to do some kind of good deeds to be saved (Acts 15:1–5). That *sounds* like common sense, but remember that God clearly explained that we are saved only by His mercy, not by our good deeds (Ephesians 2:8–9).

Don't be too quick to judge someone as a false teacher just because he teaches doctrines that your church doesn't teach. As long as he believes in the important truths of the Christian faith, minor differences are just a matter of opinion (Romans 14:1–10).

Some false teachers are like politicians who say just what people want to hear. Always be sure what a preacher says is what the Bible says!

HOW COULD THE STARS OF HEAVEN FALL TO THE EARTH?

After John saw his visions of the end of world events, he wrote down on a scroll what he had seen. Some of his visions were very unusual, but he described them as best he could. At one point, John wrote, "The stars of heaven fell to the earth, as a fig tree drops its late figs when it is shaken by a mighty wind" (Revelation 6:13 NKJV).

The Greek word *astēr* not only means "star," but also means "luminous meteor." (Our modern word *asteroid* comes from *astēr*.) John was probably describing a meteor shower, not giant stars falling.

It's also important to remember that many of John's visions weren't describing real objects but symbols of something else. For example, when John saw Jesus in a vision, Jesus was holding seven stars in His right hand, and Jesus told him, "The seven stars are the angels of the seven churches" (Revelation 1:16, 20 NKJV).

The stars in the sky fell to earth, as late figs drop from a fig tree when shaken by a strong wind.
REVELATION 6:13 NIV

WHAT IS THE GREAT TRIBULATION?.....

Jesus mentioned the Great Tribulation when He told His disciples about the end times and His second coming (Matthew 24:21). *Tribulation* means "trouble," so Jesus was warning that a time of great trouble was coming upon the earth. Even though the Great Tribulation will be a time of hardship and suffering for Christians, a great multitude will come out of it (Revelation 7:14).

> *And I said unto him, Sir, thou knowest. And he said to me, These are they which came out of great tribulation, and have washed their robes, and made them white in the blood of the Lamb.*
>
> REVELATION 7:14 KJV

Many different verses in the Bible tell us that the Tribulation will last 42 months, or 1,260 days (Revelation 11:2–3). This is about three and a half years.

Christians disagree about whether the Great Tribulation will happen soon and, if so, when it will begin. Some believe it has already happened. Others believe that it's a symbol of the suffering that Christians have had to endure down through the ages and are suffering even now in countries like China.

Christians have faced a lot of "tribulation" over the years—like when the Romans fed them to hungry animals as a form of entertainment. But many believe the "Great Tribulation" will be beyond the imagination.

DOES THE DEViL REALLY LOOK LiKE A DRAGON?

> Then another sign appeared in heaven: an enormous red dragon with seven heads and ten horns and seven crowns on its heads. . . . The great dragon was hurled down—that ancient serpent called the devil, or Satan, who leads the whole world astray. He was hurled to the earth, and his angels with him.
>
> REVELATION 12:3, 9 TNIV

This dragon statue is part of a bridge in Ljubljana, Slovenia.

John describes the devil as a giant red dragon with seven heads and a long tail, and with seven crowns, one on each head (Revelation 12:3, 9). Is this how Satan actually looks, or is it a symbol? It's a symbol.

John also describes the church as a woman, nine months pregnant, "clothed with the sun" (Revelation 12:1–2), and we know that all the people in the church don't look like *that*.

Also, John saw Jesus, the Lamb of God, as a slain lamb with seven horns and seven eyes (Revelation 5:6), and we know for certain that Jesus doesn't actually look like that. Revelation is filled with many symbols, and these are some of them.

WHAT iS THE MARK OF THE BEAST, AND WHAT DOES THE NUMBER 666 MEAN?

> And it was given to him to give breath to the image of the beast, so that the image of the beast would even speak and cause as many as do not worship the image of the beast to be killed. And he causes all, the small and the great, and the rich and the poor, and the free men and the slaves, to be given a mark on their right hand or on their forehead, and he provides that no one will be able to buy or to sell, except the one who has the mark, either the name of the beast or the number of his name. Here is wisdom. Let him who has understanding calculate the number of the beast, for the number is that of a man; and his number is six hundred and sixty-six.
>
> REVELATION 13:15–18 NASB

Many Christians today take the book of Revelation literally and believe that a dictator called the Antichrist—also known as the Beast—will arise in the near future and take over the world. The Beast will demand that everyone worship him as if he were God, and will insist that everyone receive "a mark in his right hand or on his forehead. . .which is the name of the beast or the number of his name. . . . His number is 666" (Revelation 13:16–17 NIV). People will not be able to buy or sell unless they have the mark of the Beast.

The early Christians believed that this mark would be an actual brand. Many Christians today believe it will be a miniature computer chip inserted under a person's skin.

Others say that the mark of the Beast is spiritual, representing people who worship money and materialism; they point out that Christians receive a different mark, the name of God and Christ, on their foreheads (Revelation 7:3; 9:4; 22:3–4), and this mark is surely spiritual.

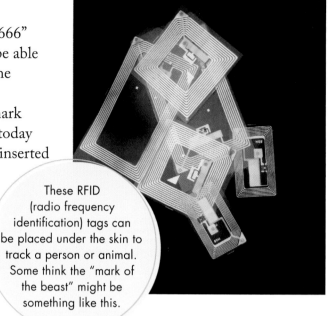

These RFID (radio frequency identification) tags can be placed under the skin to track a person or animal. Some think the "mark of the beast" might be something like this.

WHAT IS THE MILLENNIUM?

Millennium comes from the two Latin words *mille* and *ennium*, which together mean "a thousand years." The apostle John describes the Christians who went through the Great Tribulation and refused to receive the mark of the Beast, and says that "they lived and reigned with Christ a thousand years" (Revelation 20:4 KJV).

Many Christians believe that Jesus will return to this world, defeat the Antichrist and His armies in the battle of Armageddon, and set up His kingdom on earth. They also believe that this will be a tremendous time of peace when the nations will not "learn war anymore" (Isaiah 2:4 NKJV), and even animals will be at peace with each other (Isaiah 11:6–9).

Other Christians agree that Jesus will rule on earth one day but disagree when this will happen. They also say that "a thousand years" may not be literally one thousand years, but simply symbolic of a very long time.

And I saw thrones, and they sat upon them, and judgment was given unto them: and I saw the souls of them that were beheaded for the witness of Jesus, and for the word of God, and which had not worshipped the beast, neither his image, neither had received his mark upon their foreheads, or in their hands; and they lived and reigned with Christ a thousand years.

REVELATION 20:4 KJV

WHAT WILL HEAVEN BE LIKE?

John saw a vision of "the holy city, new Jerusalem" (Revelation 21:2 KJV) coming down out of the heavens, and a voice announced that God would now be living on earth among humans. Most Christians therefore believe that this heavenly city is the place where God Himself dwells, where His throne is, and that heaven itself will one day be on earth.

Revelation 21 and 22 give a beautiful, detailed description of this city, and you should read them if you want to be encouraged.

We don't know for certain if the streets will actually be made of gold that looks like transparent glass (Revelation 21:21), or whether this simply symbolizes the great beauty and riches of heaven. But we do know that we will live there forever with God and Jesus and that heaven will be wonderful and beautiful beyond our wildest dreams (1 Corinthians 2:9).

Now I saw a new heaven and a new earth, for the first heaven and the first earth had passed away. Also there was no more sea. Then I, John, saw the holy city, New Jerusalem, coming down out of heaven from God, prepared as a bride adorned for her husband. And I heard a loud voice from heaven saying, "Behold, the tabernacle of God is with men, and He will dwell with them, and they shall be His people. God Himself will be with them and be their God. And God will wipe away every tear from their eyes; there shall be no more death, nor sorrow, nor crying. There shall be no more pain, for the former things have passed away."

REVELATION 21:1–4 NKJV

GENESIS

1–2. 5
1:1 . . . . 4, 135
   (Where did God come from?)
1:14–19 5
1:26–27; 2:18–23 7
   (How were human beings created?)
1:31 5
   (Could God really create the world
   in just six days?)
2:1–3 7
   (Why did God have to rest on the
   seventh day?)
2:2 7
2:2–3 68
2:8–14 8
   (Where exactly was the Garden of
   Eden?)
2:14 8
3:20 9
4:16–17 9
   (Who was Cain's wife?)
5:5, 8, 11, 14, 17, 20, 27 9
   (Did people in ancient times
   actually live hundreds of years?)
6:15–16 10
6:19–20 10
7:7–9 10
   (How could two of every species of
   animal fit into Noah's ark?)
11:10–32 10
12:6–7 11
   (Why did God promise the
   land of Canaan to Abraham
   when it already belonged to the
   Canaanites?)
12:7 38
12:10 66
12:10–20 12
   (If Abraham was such a great man,
   why did he lie that his wife, Sarah,
   was only his sister?)
13:14–17 38
15:1 12
15:2–6 12
15:7 38
17:8 38
19:4–16 140
20:1–18 12
22:1–2 13
   (Why did God tell Abraham to
   sacrifice [kill] his son Isaac?)
25:7 10
25:23 . . . . 14, 15
   (Why did God choose Jacob over
   Esau before either son was even born?)
25:29–34 15

26:1 66
26:2–4 38
27:30–33 15
   (Why did Rebekah and Jacob
   deceive Isaac? Was it right?)
28:13–14 38
37:18–27 16
   (Why did Joseph's brothers hate
   him and sell him as a slave?)
37:31–34 16
39:11–12 126
41:53–54 66
45:4–8 16
47:28 10
50:20 136
50:26 10

EXODUS

3:1–4 17
   (Why did God appear as a burning
   a bush?)
3:2–6 26
3:5 65
3:14 18
   (Does God still speak to people out
   loud as He did to Moses?)
12. 28
13:1–2 19
13:11–15 19
   (Why was the firstborn son so
   special?)
13:20–21 26
14–15. 21
14:21–22 20
   (How did God part the Red Sea?)
15:8 20
15:22–25 35
16. 35
16:1–12 21
16:2–3 21
   (Why did the children of Israel
   complain so much right after God
   had done amazing miracles for
   them?)
17:1–7 . . . . 33, 35
19:19 18
20:3–17 22
   (Do we still need to obey the Ten
   Commandments today?)
20:5–6 23
   (Does God really punish children
   for their parents' sins?)
20:7 23
   (What does it mean to take God's
   name in vain?)
20:8–10 24
   (Why do some Christians rest

on Saturday and others rest on
Sunday?)
20:8–11 7
20:12 132
20:17 101
21:2 72
21:22–25 101
23:16 19
23:27–31 41
23:32–33 34
25:10–11 25
   (What was the ark of the covenant,
   and what made it so special?)
25:12–15 65
25:22 . . . . 25, 50
26:1 25
   (What was the tabernacle?)
28:41 53
32:1–14 96
33:7–11 . . . . 17, 26
33:18–23 18
33:20–23 26
33:23 26
   (Does God have a body like we
   do?)
34:11 41
34:19 19

LEVITICUS

1:1 27
   (Why did God give the Israelites so
   many rules and laws to follow?)
4 28
4:29 28
   (After they had sinned, why did
   the Israelites have to sacrifice an
   animal?)
11. 93
11:46–47 28
   (Why did the Israelites have so
   many rules about food, and why
   don't Christians follow these dietary
   laws today?)
12:6–8 19
13. 36
14:33–57 36
17:1–7 33
17:10–14 93
17:11 28
18:24–25 41
18:24–28 11
19:11 39
19:31 85
20:6 85
23:1–2 29
   (Why did the Israelites have to
   celebrate so many festivals each year?)

23:32–33 34
25:23 11
25:25 48
25:35–37 58
25:39–43 72
27:3–5 30
(Were men worth more than women in Old Testament times?)

NUMBERS

1:1–2 . . . . 31, 56
(Why did God tell Moses to count only the men who came out of Egypt?)
1:3 31
4:15 65
6:1–8 32
(What is a Nazirite?)
11:4–9, 31–32 35
13–14. 31
14:26–31 38
20:1–13 35
20:10 33
20:12 33
(Why didn't God allow Moses to enter the Promised Land just because Moses lost his temper one time?)
22:28 33
(How was Balaam's donkey able to talk?)
26. 31
26:1–2 56
33:52 34
(What are "high places," and what was so bad about them?)

DEUTERONOMY

3:23–27 33
6:6 141
7:1 41
7:3–4 70
8:3–4 35
(How did the Israelites survive in the desert for 40 years?)
12:2–14 34
12:5–14 70
14:28–29 58
15:1–11 58
17:17 59
22:10 129
23:12–14 36
(How did the Israelites keep from getting sick when they knew nothing about germs and disease?)
23:15–16 139

23:21 45
26:12–13 37
(Are Christians today supposed to tithe?)
28. . . . . 74, 87

JOSHUA

1:5–6 38
1:6 38
(Why was Canaan called the Promised Land?)
2:4–6 39
(Why did God bless Rahab the prostitute even though she told a lie?)
2:8–11 39
2:11 41
3:13 39
(How did the Jordan River part?)
3:16 40
6 40
6:20 40
(How did the walls of Jericho fall down?)
6:21 41
(Why did God tell the Israelites to kill the Canaanitesmen, women, and children? Wasn't that totally cruel?)
6:25 39
9:24 41
10:1–5 41
10:12–13 41
(Did the sun actually stand still when Joshua prayed that it would?)
10:13 42
11:18–19 42
(Why were there so many wars and killings in the Old Testament? Why didn't the Israelites just love their enemies like Jesus said?)

JUDGES

2:11 43
(Who was Baal, and why did the Israelites worship him?)
4:1–8 80
6:7–10 44
6:13 44
(Why did God do such huge miracles in olden days but doesn't do them today?)
6:15 44
(If Gideon was so fearful and doubting, how did he become such a great hero?)

11:35–36 45
(Why did Jephthah have to keep his vow to sacrifice his daughter?)
13:3–5 32
13:4–5 46
14:6 46
15:14 46
16:17–20 46
(Why did Samson lose all his strength just because of a haircut?)

RUTH

1:16–17 47
2:10–12 47
3:3 53
3:10 47
(Was Ruth conniving and greedy for going after a rich, older man?)
3:12 48
(What is a kinsman redeemer?)
4 48
4:12 48
(Why was it so important in Old Testament days to have children?)
4:15 48

1 SAMUEL

1:8 48
1:11 49
(Where did the practice of dedicating children come from?)
1:24–28 49
2:12–17 50
2:18–19 49
2:27–30 50
3:13 50
4:3 50
4:10–11 50
(If the ark of the covenant was so special, why did God allow the Philistines to capture it?)
5–6. 50
6:19–20 65
8:1–5 . . . . 50, 51
(Why did the sons of such a godly man as Samuel turn out bad?)
9:2 51
10:21–24 51
11:6–11 51
13:1–13 51
13:13–14 51
(King Saul was such a great leader in the beginning. Why did he end up failing so miserably?)
13:14 52
14:47–48 51

15:1–31 51
15:17 51
15:22 52
(What did Samuel mean when he said, "Obedience is better than sacrifice"?)
16:1 53
16:12 52
(What made King David Israel's greatest leader?)
16:13 53
(What does it mean to be anointed?)
17:4–7 53
17:40 53
(Why did David take five stones when he went to fight Goliath, when he only needed one to kill him?)
17:50–51 53
18:1–12 51
28. 52
28:5–19 85
30. 52

2 SAMUEL

1:1–16 64
1:18 42
1:23 42
2:1–9 54
5:1–3 54
5:17–25 54
8 56
8:1 54
(Why did David fight so many wars?)
10. 54
11:27 55
(How did David get away with stealing another man's wife and killing the man?)
12:11–19 55
13. 55
14:25–26 56
15–20. 54
15:1–6 56
15:10 55
(Why did Absalom rebel against his father, King David, and try to become king in his place?)
18. 55
21. 66
22:15 75
24:1 56
24:2 56
(Why was it such a sin for David to count how many soldiers he had in his army?)

24:13–16 10

1 KINGS

3:9 . . . . 57, 80
3:12 57
(Can I pray for great wisdom and get it like King Solomon did?)
3:16–28 57
6:21 58
(Why was the temple completely covered with gold inside? Shouldn't that gold have been used to care for the poor?)
8:27 . . . . 58, 59
(Did God actually live in the temple that Solomon built?)
8:29 58
11:1 59
(Why did God let Solomon have 700 wives?)
11:2 70
11:3–4 59
11:3–9 70
17:22–23 60
(How come Christians today don't do great miracles like Elijah and other Old Testament prophets?)
18:28 43
18:41–45 97
19:12 18

2 KINGS

2:23–24 61
(Why did God send bears to kill some little children when all they did was tease Elisha?)
4:1 72
6:6 62
(How did God make an iron ax head float?)
7:6 62
(Does God ever trick people into thinking that something is true when it really isn't?)
8:16–22 67
10:17 63
(Were all the violent things King Jehu did good or bad?)
10:30 63
18:1–7 51
21:1–11 51
22:1–2 51

1 CHRONICLES

10:1–6 64

10:4 64
(Why does the Bible give two different stories of how King Saul died?)
13:6–12 65
(Why was Uzzah killed for merely trying to keep the ark of the covenant from tipping over?)
15:1–2 65
21:1 56
29:1–9 58

2 CHRONICLES

2:6 . . . . 26, 58
6:26–27 66
(Are droughts and famines God's judgment on sin?)
21. 67
21:4 67
(How could King Jehoram be so cruel as to kill all his brothers?)
21:13 67
24:17 67
(How could good King Joash turn against God so quickly and so totally?)
29:21 68
(Why is the number seven so special?)
36:16 68
(If we keep on sinning, does there come a point at which there is no more hope of repentance and mercy?)

EZRA

1:1 69
(Why did Persia's King Cyrus allow the Jews to return to their homeland?)
1:3 70
(Why was it so important for the Jews to rebuild the temple?)
3:1–10 70
3:8–10 98
4:23–24 98
9:1–2 70
(Why was Ezra so angry about Jews marrying non-Jews?)
9:11 11

NEHEMIAH

1:3 71
3:1–5 71
(Why was it so important to build a wall around Jerusalem?)

5:1–5 72
  (Why did some parents in Old
  Testament times sell their children
  as slaves?)
5:1–12 72
13:26 70

ESTHER

1–10 73
  (Why is God never mentioned in
  the book of Esther?)
2:12 53
4:15–16 73

JOB

1:1–12 74
1:21 89
1:21–22 74
  (Why did God allow Job to suffer so
  much?)
2:1–7 74
2:9 74
3 91
9 91
30:19 78
31:1 101
32:1–3 74
  (Were Job's three friends right when
  they said that God was judging Job
  for his sins?)
42:12–16 74

PSALMS

5:5–6 75
  (If God is love, why do the Psalms
  say that God hates evildoers?)
10:1–13 76
10:15 76
  (Why did David pray mean prayers,
  such as, "God, break the arms of the
  wicked"?)
20 56
34:10 77
34:17 76
  (If you truly love God, will He keep
  all trouble out of your life?)
34:19 76
37:4 77
  (Will God always supply everything
  we want?)
39:1 101
41:9 114
73:3–20 137
89:38–51 89
89:52 89

90:2 4
90:10 10
91:11 . . . . 103, 140
95:7–8 141
102:10 78
  (Would God really "cast away"
  someone who believes in Him?)
102:27 4
103:8–10 96
104:15 53
106:32–33 33
112:1 78
  (Why should we fear God? Isn't He
  our loving Father?)
114:3–7 40
127:3–5 48
139:7–10 26
147:5 5
150 79
  (Why do the Psalms tell us over and
  over to praise God? Does God enjoy
  hearing us constantly tell Him how
  great He is?)

PROVERBS

4:7 . . . . 80, 82
  (What is wisdom?)
4:14–15 126
9:10 79
13:1 51
24:29 101
31 80
31:30 80
  (Should modern women and girls
  behave like women of ancient
  times?)

ECCLESIASTES

1:2 81
  (Why is Ecclesiastes such a sad,
  discouraging book?)
1:14 81
1:18 82
  (If knowledge brings grief and
  sorrow, why go to school?)
2:10 59
3:1 82
  (Why does Solomon say that there
  are times to kill, to tear down, and to
  hate?)
3:2, 4, 7 82
3:16–17 82
4:1–3 82
5:3, 7 95
12:13–14 81

SONG OF SONGS

1:1–3 83
  (Why did Solomon write a book all
  about romance?)

ISAIAH

2:2 84
2:3 84
  (What is the mountain of the Lord's
  house?)
2:4 150
6 104
8:19 85
  (What does the Bible say about
  going to mediums?)
9:6 115
11:6–9 150
19:3–4 85
29:6 40
29:8 95
40:28 7
43:10 4
45:1–4, 13 69
45:12, 18 6
46:4 4
53:1 86
53:4–5 86
  (Why do people say that Isaiah 53 is
  a prophecy about Jesus?)
53:5 89
53:7–8 86
59:1–2 86
  (If people won't stop sinning, does
  God refuse to hear their prayers?)
65:2–4 43

JEREMIAH

1:14–16 87
1:15 87
  (Why did God let the pagan
  Babylonians conquer His own
  people, the Jews?)
3:10 87
12:2 87
20:7 87
  (Why didn't the Jews listen to the
  prophet Jeremiah?)
28 87
31:31–33 127
32:35 46
36:9 73
38:4–6 67
44:15–18 87

LAMENTATIONS

2:19 88
(If God is all-powerful, why does He allow children to suffer?)
3:1–5 89
(Is it okay to complain to God when we pray?)
3:1–36 89

EZEKIEL

1:4–14 90
1:5 90
(What are cherubim?)
4 93
5 93
10:1–17 90
12 91
12:5–12 91
(Why did the prophet Ezekiel do so many strange things?)
12:11 91
18:1–9 23
18:1–23 96
24:15–27 91
37:7–10 92
(What does Ezekiel's weird vision about dry bones mean?)
37:11 92
38:18–20 40

DANIEL

1:8, 11–12 93
(Why did Daniel and his friends refuse to eat food from the king's table?)
2:45 94
(What do Daniel's visions and prophecies mean?)
3:1–18 123
6:1–13 123
6:16 94
(How did Daniel survive in a den full of lions?)
6:22 94
7:1 95
(Does God still speak to people in dreams and visions?)
9:25 71
10:12–13 104

JONAH

1:17 96
(Did Jonah really spend three days and three nights in the belly of a great fish?)

3 96
3:10 96
(Does God actually change His mind about things?)

HABAKKUK

1:2–3 97
(Why does God sometimes take so long to answer our prayers?)

HAGGAI

1 66
1:7–8 98
(Will God refuse to bless us if we don't give money to the church?)

MALACHI

3:8–12 37

MATTHEW

1:5 39
1:18–20 99
1:20–21 140
1:24–25 99
(How could a virgin become pregnant?)
3:1–2 100
(What does it mean to repent?)
3:13–15 120
3:17 115
4:8–10 144
4:11 140
5:11–12 118
5:29 100
(Why did Jesus say, "If your right eye causes you to sin, pluck it out and throw it away"?)
5:38–39 101
5:39 . . . . 42, 101
(What did Jesus mean when He said, "Resist not evil"? Are we supposed to let people walk all over us?)
5:44 . . . . 42, 102
5:45 . . . . 66, 102
5:48 102
(Does Jesus really expect us to be perfect?)
6:1–2 113
6:5 113
6:7 102
(Why did Jesus say not to use "vain repetitions" when we pray, yet He prayed the exact same words three different times?)

6:19–21 81
6:25–26 103
(Does Jesus really want us to be like the birds and not work at all or save any money, but just trust Him to supply our needs?)
7:12 127
7:15–20 146
10:5–6 107
12:40 96
13:3–8 141
13:18–23 141
13:58 44
15:21–28 107
17:1–8 131
18:10 . . . . 103, 104
(Do we all have guardian angels who constantly watch over us?)
19:3–8 139
21:21–22 104
(Did Jesus really mean it when He said that if we believe when we pray, we'll receive whatever we pray for?)
22:36–40 . . . . 22, 24
22:37 79
23 116
23:6–7 113
23:14 113
24 105
24:21 148
24:30–31 136
24:36 136
24:42 105
(Are we living in the end times?)
25:31–40 89
26:24 114
26:26–28 126
26:38–39 114
27:12–14 86
27:18 113
27:50–54 40
28:1–4 109
28:2 40
28:6 105
(How did Jesus rise from the dead?)

MARK

1:8 106
(What does it mean to be baptized with the Holy Spirit?)
1:10 112
1:15 100
1:29–31, 40–42 108
3:1–5 108
3:5 107
(How could Jesus have never sinned when the Bible says that He sometimes got angry?)

5:25–29 .108
7:3–4 36
7:24–30 .107
7:26–27 .107
(Why did Jesus ignore the
Phoenician woman when she
begged Him to help her?)
9:23 . . . . 45, 105
9:25 108
(Is the devil responsible for causing
all sickness and disease?)
9:25–26 .108
9:43–44 .111
(If God is love, why would He send
someone to a place as horrible as hell?)
9:48 108
10:21 121
14:32–41 103
16:1–7 109
16:5 109
(Why does Mark say that the
women saw one angel inside Jesus'
tomb, but Luke says the women
saw two angels there? Is that a
contradiction?)
16:9 123
16:9–14 .110
(Why didn't Jesus' disciples believe
at first that He had risen from the
dead?)

LUKE

1:1–4 111
(Why are there four Gospels?)
1:26–33 .123
1:34–35 99
1:35 112
(Who is the Holy Spirit?)
2:22–24 19
3:8–14 100
3:14 112
(If John the Baptist told the Roman
soldiers to "do violence to no man,"
how can Christians be police officers
or soldiers?)
6:22–23 .118
6:38 37
8:1–3 123
11:42 113
(Why were the Pharisees so focused
on obeying tiny little laws?)
12:11–12 117
18:1 97
19:47 113
(Why were the religious leaders
of Israel so offended by what Jesus
taught and did?)
22:3 114

(Why did Jesus pick a disciple
(Judas) who would betray Him?)
22:19 126
22:24–26 113
22:31–34 .74
22:42–44 140
22:44 103
23:43 143
24:1–7 109
24:11 110
24:39–40 114
(What kind of body did Jesus have
after His resurrection?)

JOHN

1:1 . . . . 115, 135
(Is Jesus God's Son, or is He God
Himself?)
1:14 . . . . 115, 132, 135
1:29 . . . . 22, 28
3:6 . . . . 116, 117
3:7 116
(What did Jesus mean when He
said, "You must be born again"?)
3:16 . . . . 75, 130, 144
4:19–24 59
4:24 26
5:39 131
6:63 116
7:24 116
(Why are there so many hypocrites
in the church?)
10:30 115
10:41 60
11:38–44 105
12:28–29 .18
12:38 86
13:18 114
14:6 117
(Is Jesus the only way to God?)
14:26 117
(What does the Holy Spirit do?)
15:18–21 118
(Why do Christians suffer
persecution?)
16:7 117
16:13 112
17:1–5 119
17:5 134
17:11 119
(If Jesus was God, why did He pray
to God? Wasn't He just talking to
Himself?)
19:33–35 . . . . 110, 143
20:1 24
20:24–27 114
20:24–28 110
21:24 143

ACTS

1:8 117
2:1–4 106
2:14 74
2:38 . . . . 100, 120, 143
(Why is it so important to be
baptized?)
2:44–45 .121
(Are Christians supposed to give
up all their money and worldly
possessions?)
4:12 117
4:18–20 .123
5:17–25 .140
6–7 118
7:48 58
8:14–17 .106
8:32–33 86
9:1–9 129
10:9–16 29
10:13–15, 28 29
12:11–12 123
12:15 104
13:22 52
14:19 129
14:22 76
15:1 131
15:1–5 146
16:16–24 129
16:30–31 121
16:31 . . . . 121, 142
(What does it mean to believe in
Jesus Christ?)
17:5 129
18:1–3, 18 123
19:1–6 106
20:7 24
20:29–30 138
21:27–34 134
23:11 134
24:26 134
26:9–11 75
27:23–24 140

ROMANS

1:3–4 105
1:16 107
3:23 . . . . 75, 122
(Is everybody in the world a sinner
even good, moral people?)
4:18–22 12
5:5 128
5:8 . . . . 75, 127
6:23 122
(How is salvation a free gift?)
8:9 . . . . 106, 112
8:11 105

8:15 130
8:16 117
8:28 136
9:10–12 14
10:9–10 .142
12:17–21 .101
13:1 123
(Are we supposed to submit to governments and authorities even when they're wrong?)
13:4 . . . . 42, 123
13:8–10 22
14:1–3 29
14:1–10 146
15:13 117
15:24, 28 .134
15:26 98
16:1 123
(Were there outstanding women in the New Testament?)
16:1–2 123
16:3 123
16:3–5 98

1 CORINTHIANS

1:11–13 .124
(Christians have many different doctrines and churches. Is that wrong?)
1:27, 29 14
2:9 151
2:10–11 112
3:11–15 125
(When we get to heaven, will we be rewarded for our good deeds and punished for our bad deeds?)
6:18 . . . . 125, 126
(Why does the Bible tell us to flee sexual immorality?)
7:21 139
10:19–20 . . . . 23, 34
11:5–6 80
11:23–26 .126
(What is the purpose of Communion?)
11:24–26 77
11:25 127
(What does "new testament" mean?)
13. 127
(Who can have as much love as the Bible says we're supposed to have? Isn't that unrealistic?)
14:34 80
15. 128
15:20–23 .128
(What does the Bible mean when it says that we will be resurrected?)
15:42–44 .114

16:2 24

2 CORINTHIANS

4:10 129
(Why was the apostle Paul beaten up so much?)
4:13 79
5:10 125
6:14 129
(What does it mean not to be unequally yoked with unbelievers?)
6:18 130
(How can we be sons and daughters of God? Isn't Jesus God's one and only Son?)
8:12 98
9:6–8 . . . . 37, 98
11:24–26 77
12:7 130
(What was Paul's "thorn in the flesh"?)

GALATIANS

3:1–2 131
(Why did Paul write so much about trusting in Jesus instead of religously obeying the Law of Moses?)
3:28 80
4:4–6 130
4:6 . . . . 106, 117
4:15 130
5:22 128
5:22–23 117
6:11 130

EPHESIANS

1:13–14 .106
2:8 132
(What is grace?)
2:8–9 146
4:3–6 124
4:26 107
4:28 121
6:1 132
6:1–4 132
(How should children treat their parents?)
6:11–17 .133
(What is the armor of God?)

PHILIPPIANS

1:12 134
(Why was Paul in prison?)
2:6–7 134
(Did Jesus give up His power as God when He came to earth?)

2:14 89
3:20–21 .128
4:2–3 123
4:6 89
4:11–12 78
4:19 78

COLOSSIANS

1:15–16 .135
(How is Jesus Christ different from every other famous man who started a religion?)
3:18 80
4:1 139

1 THESSALONIANS

2:18 136
(How come Satan is allowed to hinder God's plans?)
4:14–17 .128
4:17 136
(What is the Rapture?)

2 THESSALONIANS

2:3–4 145

1 TIMOTHY

1:15 75
2:12 80
6:6–9 78
6:7 81
6:9 137
(Is it wrong to be rich?)
6:17–18 .137

2 TIMOTHY

1:7 12
3:12 129
3:16 137
(What does it mean that the Bible is inspired by God?)

TITUS

3:10 138
(What is heresy?)

PHILEMON

15–16. 139
(In the Bible, a Christian named Philemon owned a slave. Does that mean God approves of slavery?)

HEBREWS

1:13–14 140
  (What do angels do?)
3:15 141
  (What does it mean to harden your heart?)
9:4 25
9:22 28
10:11–14 131
12:5–6 141
  (Why does God allow us to go through hard times?)
12:10–11 141
13:5 78

JAMES

1:5 57
1:6–7 104
2:14 142
  (Why does James say that simply believing God is not enough? Doesn't this contradict what Paul taught?)
2:15–16 88
2:17 142
2:19 121
5:1–6 137
5:14 53

1 PETER

1:18–19 22
3:7 80
3:20–21 143
3:21 . . . . 120, 143
  (Do you need to be baptized in order to be saved?)
5:8 136

2 PETER

1:16 143
  (How can we be sure that the stories about Jesus are true?)
1:21 137
2:18–19 146

1 JOHN

1:1 . . . . 143, 145
1:7 . . . . 120, 143
2:15–17 144
  (God loves the world, and we are told to imitate God. Why then are we warned _not_ to love the world?)
2:16 100

2:18 145
  (What does the word _antichrist_ mean?)
3:2 128
3:17–18 88
3:18 142
4:2–3 145
  (Who were the Gnostics?)
4:8 75
4:20 133
5:1–3 142
5:14–15 104

JUDE

4 146
  (How can we know when someone is a false teacher?)

REVELATION

1:12, 16 68
1:13–15 134
1:14–16 114
1:16, 20 147
4:5 68
4:6–9 90
5:1 68
5:6 68
5:11–12 140
6:10–11 . . . . 97, 104
6:13 147
  (How could the stars of heaven fall to the earth?)
7:3 150
7:14 148
  (What is the Great Tribulation?)
8:6 68
9:4 150
11:2–3 148
12:1–2 149
12:3, 9 149
  (Does the devil really look like a dragon?)
12:7–8 136
12:11 94
13 145
13:15–18 149
  (What is the mark of the Beast, and what does the number 666 mean?)
13:16–17 150
15:1 68
20:4 150
  (What is the Millennium?)
20:15 108
21 151
21:1–4 151
  (What will heaven be like?)

21:21 151
22 151
22:3–4 150